T0355285

Run for Elected Office— and Win

Jana M. Kemp

Apress®

Run for Elected Office—and Win

Copyright © 2012 by Jana M. Kemp

All rights reserved. No part of this work may be reproduced or transmitted in any form or by any means, electronic or mechanical, including photocopying, recording, or by any information storage or retrieval system, without the prior written permission of the copyright owner and the publisher.

ISBN-13 (pbk): 978-1-4302-3798-3

ISBN-13 (electronic): 978-1-4302-3800-3

Printed and bound in the United States of America 9 8 7 6 5 4 3 2 1

Trademarked names may appear in this book. Rather than use a trademark symbol with every occurrence of a trademarked name, we use the names only in an editorial fashion and to the benefit of the trademark owner, with no intention of infringement of the trademark.

President and Publisher: Paul Manning
Lead Editor: Jeff Olson
Development Editor: Robert Hutchinson
Editorial Board: Steve Anglin, Mark Beckner, Ewan Buckingham, Gary Cornell, Morgan Ertel, Jonathan Gennick, Jonathan Hassell, Robert Hutchinson, Michelle Lowman, James Markham, Matthew Moodie, Jeff Olson, Jeffrey Pepper, Douglas Pundick, Ben Renow-Clarke, Dominic Shakeshaft, Gwenan Spearing, Matt Wade, Tom Welsh
Editorial Assistant: Rita Fernando
Copy Editors: Debra Adams
Compositor: Mary Sudul
Indexer: SPi Global
Cover Designer: Anna Ishchenko

Distributed to the book trade worldwide by Springer-Verlag New York, Inc., 233 Spring Street, 6th Floor, New York, NY 10013. Phone 1-800-SPRINGER, fax 201-348-4505, e-mail orders-ny@springer-sbm.com, or visit http://www.springeronline.com.

For information on translations, please contact us by e-mail at info@apress.com, or visit http://www.apress.com.

Apress and friends of ED books may be purchased in bulk for academic, corporate, or promotional use. eBook versions and licenses are also available for most titles. For more information, reference our Special Bulk Sales–eBook Licensing web page at http://www.apress.com/info/bulksales.

The information in this book is distributed on an "as is" basis, without warranty. Although every precaution has been taken in the preparation of this work, neither the author(s) nor Apress shall have any liability to any person or entity with respect to any loss or damage caused or alleged to be caused directly or indirectly by the information contained in this work.

Through 4-H program participation, I was introduced to the importance of community and civic service. While standing in the U.S. Capitol in Washington, D.C. as a teenager, I was inspired to run for elected office.

Seven generations of my family have been involved in U.S. public service, from fighting in the Revolutionary War to holding elected office. My family members modeled public and community service while I was growing up, and have continued to be supporters, fans, consolers, and best of all—my family!

My immediate family is to be credited for their creativity, grace, and patience during my 2010 Independent race for Governor of Idaho. I am grateful for their continued love and support.

Contents

About the Author

Jana M. Kemp represented District 16B (Garden City and parts of Northwest Boise) in the Idaho House of Representatives, 2004–06, where she served on the Transportation, Education, Local Government, Commerce, Human Resources, and Responsible Budgeting committees. During the 2010 election cycle, she ran as an independent for governor of Idaho, placing third in the five-candidate field.

Jana is a small business owner. She founded Meeting & Management Essentials in 1993 in Minnesota and, in 1994, moved the company to Idaho, where she received the following honors: 2010 Trailblazer, National Association of Women Business Owners of Boise and Southern Idaho; 2006 Women of the Year, *Idaho Business Review*; 2001 Accomplished Under 40, *Idaho Business Journal*; 1999 Integrity Counts Small Business Award, Better Business Bureau; and 1996 Entrepreneur of the Year, Alpha Kappa Psi. Her clients include Fortune 100 companies, non-profits, trade associations, and government agencies. Jana is the author of five books on management and community service, which have been translated into numerous languages: *No!—How One Simple Word Can Transform Your Life*, *Prepared Not Paranoid*, *Moving Meetings*, *Moving Out of the Box*, and *Building Community in Buildings*. She was a business columnist for the *Idaho Press Tribune* and *Idaho Business Review,* and hosted a business-radio talk show for four years.

Jana has served as an officer and volunteer in many service organizations, including Learning Lab, the Idaho State Bar Association Public Information Committee, the Idaho State Association of Parliamentarians, the American Society of Training and Development, Easter Seals, Goodwill, and Senior Solutions. Jana is also a graduate of the Citizen Law Academy, the Citizen Police Academy, and the Idaho POST Police Academy. She lives in Idaho with her husband and step-daughter.

Acknowledgments

Thanks to Jeff Olson at Apress for championing this book from idea to reality. Thanks also go to the Apress team for introducing me to their electronic publishing system, and to Robert Hutchinson and Rita Fernando for their final edits that strengthened the book.

Most of all, I want to thank the teams of people who supported me in 2004 and 2006, and the amazing 2010 Vote Kemp Team that formed around the cause of seeing an independent and capable candidate become governor of Idaho. I am grateful that the team stayed true to the cause of shedding light on the darkness at work in state politics, so that voters can see what is at work in state politics. May the light keep shining on all elected officials and candidates for office! Americans need to know for whom they are casting their votes.

Introduction

"Why did you decide to run for office?" This is the question I get asked most often when speaking to groups about public service. The next question is, "Are you going to run again?"

My aha! moment of inspiration to run for elected government office came to me in 1982, when I was a teenager on a 4-H trip to Washington, D.C. Standing in the U.S. Capitol rotunda, looking at the history on the walls, soaking in its solemn majesty, and admiring the monumental architecture, I was struck by a sense of the sacred mission of serving as one the people's chosen representatives. The charged atmosphere spoke to many of us Minnesotan 4-Hers on that trip: one of us went on to run for U.S. Senate; another became speaker of the house in her state and ran for governor in 2010. I went on to serve as a state legislator in the Idaho House of Representatives (2004-2006), and then run in 2006 for a second term, which the voters opted not to give me. This loss created space for my 2010 independent run for governor of Idaho.

My predisposition to public service was formed from infancy by my parents, who met when my father was serving in the U.S. Army and my mother was working for the Kentucky Extension Service. Both my parents instilled in me the conviction that our American republic can survive and flourish only if good, just, honest, capable, ordinary citizens heed the patriotic call to present themselves for public service, as my ancestors did in the Revolutionary War.

The earliest example in my life that I can remember of taking up the fight for justice dates to elementary school in Indiana in 1976. I earned my way onto the boys' basketball team, taking all kinds of heat from boys and girls in the process. By the end of junior high school, our family had helped my father campaign for a school board position in Minnesota, and I had run twice for student body council offices. During the school assembly speeches in one of my races, a boy campaigning for the same office said, "And she plans to paint the bathrooms pink"—which was an outright lie. Another year my pains-takingly homemade campaign signs were torn off the walls. A wise friend who had stayed after school to help put up these signs counseled me, "Don't let them win. Just keep putting the signs back up." In 2004, 2006, and 2010, I repeated this advice to my campaign team members who were upset about disappearing signs: "Just put the signs right back up."

During junior high and high school, I participated in 4-H programs and club meetings. I served in the elected positions of treasurer, secretary, reporter, vice president, president, and county officer positions. In high school, I ran for president of the Honor Society. I talked to every person in the society whom I knew and asked them to vote for me. The day of the election, the vice principal called me into her office. "We've counted the ballots and counted them again," she said. "We've never seen this happen before. You've lost the race by just two votes." Of course, I was deeply frustrated, and spoke to people asking whether they'd remembered to vote. I found out that three people who knew me well, and whom I had asked for their votes, hadn't voted. Lesson learned: ask, ask, and ask again, and remind people to vote for you as they may not otherwise remember to even cast a ballot.

Over the years of early adulthood, I ran for and held my college's student body academic head position, neighborhood association offices, trade association positions, precinct committeeman, and elected office in volunteer organizations. Each of these service terms provided opportunities to learn about group process, decision making, and the need for social interactions along with business task accomplishments that most human beings need in order to stay involved in an organization.

These positions and school-days campaign experiences taught me the rudiments of parliamentary procedure, business organization, and served as the foundations for the business that I founded in 1993, Meeting & Management Essentials. In my early thirties, to expand my knowledge of parliamentary process, I became a member of the National Association of Parliamentarians.

Being involved in the community is what helps you to build your understanding of the area you wish to serve. Being involved in a variety of organizations and positions also helps you to build name recognition—which you'll most definitely need if you want to win the race you enter.

For example:

From 1996 to July 2009, I wrote regular business columns for the *Idaho Business Review* (distributed statewide) and for the *Idaho Press Tribune* (distributed in the county adjacent to the one in which I live). These columns helped me gain insight into our state's business community and gain name recognition around the state.

From 1998 to 2002, I originated and hosted a live business talk radio program on Idaho's only 50,000 watt station (which means it covers about one third of our state). To this day, people will say, "Didn't you used to be on the radio?" During these same years, I provided periodic business tips on the highest-rated morning news show in our market.

In 1999, I participated in the Citizen Police Academy to learn about the workings of the local police department. This experience gave me insight into the law enforcement community in a way that just living in the community doesn't. I also met people who became supporters in the state races I would go on to run. In 2000, I participated in the Citizen Law Academy to learn about the state's judicial and legal system. This experience provided insight into the judicial branch of government and became the basis for my citizen service on the Idaho State Bar Association's Public Information Committee. In 2002, I graduated from a ten-week course at the Idaho Police Academy, prerequisite to becoming a sworn police officer. This experience raised my level of awareness about my personal safety, the safety of every community member, and the threats of drug addiction in today's society. Police academy experience led to contracts for my business and became the basis for my book, *Prepared Not Paranoid.*

In March 2004, someone said to me, "Jana, did you know there is an open House seat in your district? Why don't you run?" It was the beginning of the two-week filing period, so I didn't have much time to make a decision. I did my research and jumped into a tough Republican primary race. I'll share more of the story in the pages ahead.

If you already know you are running for office or are interested in holding public office, this book will help you. If your heart is in public service for a good greater than yourself, this book is absolutely for you.

At the end of any given race, sometimes you will have won and gained the elected position. Sometimes you will not gain the position you sought, and yet the run will still qualify as a win because you and your team were able to demonstrate integrity, honesty, and intelligence, and to raise the standards of public discourse and public expectations.

Stay tuned as to whether I'll run again. In the meantime:

Run for Elected Office—and Win!

Jana Kemp
Boise, Idaho
January 2012

Run for It

Why the Future Depends on You

Every election has the potential to change people's lives, to affect the way a community operates, to determine the way a business might grow, to define what will happen in our children's schools, to outline what can happen in the county or state, to address the needs of people, and to etch indelibly into our souls a sense of safety and security or a sense of danger and corruption. In today's world, citizens are hungry for a sense of security in their everyday lives. They want to see their hopes realized by—rather than continually disappointed by—their elected officials. Elected officials' poor decision making and behavior in the public and personal arenas lead to citizen disenchantment with the value of voting and disgust with anything related to government. In today's world, protests and marches register dissent with governments. As in the past, concern for the future is driven by what is and is not happening in the present.

The level of concern, frustration, and disenfranchisement that exists today indicates our country's need for improved governance from elected officials at all levels. This far-reaching need for better leadership is why the future depends on your decision to run for elected office. This book will help you discover whether your thoughts about running for office are worth pursuing. We need more good people—especially people who view elected office as a public service rather than as a life-time career. The Founding Fathers envisioned an America in which elected office was a duty and privilege with positions to be filled for a time. Then, after completing the term of office, a person's lifetime profession would be resumed.

Opportunity exists. At any given moment, there are about two million elected officials in elected positions in the United States of America. The exact number is difficult to pinpoint, owing to the abundance of elected positions in the labyrinthine matrix of levels, branches, and departments that constitutes American government. Levels of government, each with nested interdependencies but competing sovereignty and prerogative claims, range across federal, state, county, city, township, village, tribal reservation, and special district (such as various school, zoning, management, and conservation districts). Branches and departments range across legislative, executive, judicial, fiscal, administrative, legal, medical, and law enforcement jurisdictions. Then there are the on-the-ballot elections for political party and other such positions. As an American citizen, you have virtually infinite opportunities to serve in elected office.

If you are looking for a book about how to become an elected public servant for a portion of your life, then this book is for you. *Run for Elected Office—and Win* will tell you everything you need to know: how to select the office that is a good match for your interests and skills; how to plan and run your campaign; and how to survive the election, whether you win or lose. In the chapters ahead you'll learn the ins and outs of an election from an author who's done it and won—and done it and lost. We'll begin by pinpointing your passion for service and identify the position that matches that passion. Then you'll explore whether you want to declare a party affiliation and how that fits into your selection of a position. Along the way, you will discover tips for saying what you mean and attracting media attention. You'll learn how much money it takes to run and what it takes to win.

Why the Future Depends on You

The future of representative democracy in America depends on you—because if you don't run, then who will? Yes, I hear you sighing, "My neighbor … or that guy with more money than I have … or even the #@$%*! who's been in office all these years." These alternatives reflect exactly why you are needed. Most people in America are saying the same thing and waiting for someone else to address the problems that are frustrating us all and to present some new ideas and choices that would benefit us all. Worse, more and more citizens are just tuning out the non-stop media barrage of inane political rhetoric, staged histrionics, and permanent campaigning. When it comes time to vote, many are too jaded to bother.

On the upside, there are unmistakable signs of a swelling popular revolt against the ethos of impotent resignation: Tea Party and Occupy Wall Street grassroots activists, union supporters, independents, and interest groups of many stripes are all pouring into the streets and state capitols to shout their unhappiness with politics as usual. They have decided to act.

You can do the same. Rather than abdicating your personal autonomy and giving up on your family's and children's future, discover what position is a good match for you to pursue (more on this in Chapters 2 and 3) and go for it.

If you think that money is a barrier to running for office, you may discover that money is not the challenge. True, presidential races involve millions of dollars. President Obama's 2008 election spending was a record $740 million. And yet there are local elections that are still regularly won with as little as $100. Don't let money be the barrier to your entering a race. (More on this in Chapter 8.)

Do you find yourself agreeing with the idea, "Why run when the incumbent has such a lock on the seat?" Maybe it is time for the incumbent to be ushered out of office and you are just the one who can do it. You may determine that the incumbent's name recognition and ratings are so high that his or her seat may not be the best seat to run for at this time. That is perfectly OK. There are dozens of other elected offices you might choose to run for in order to prepare yourself for the seat you first had in mind. In the meantime, you can gain experience and watch for signals that the incumbent is retiring or weakening.

Another way to help you decide whether a run for office is worth the effort is to research how well the people in elected office are informed about the issues you care about. Start doing your homework. Consider my first run for elected public office. In 2004, I heard reports of House Education Committee members discussing children and learning by saying things like, "We all know that children don't learn until they are six." My reaction was, "Are they kidding? Didn't they watch their own children grow up? Never mind that research over the last twenty years has proven how much children learn *before* the age of six. Are they not even paying attention to their children and grandchildren growing up?" Such cavalier displays of ignorance, indolence, and incuriosity in my legislators compelled me to run for office.

America needs reasonable, realistic, and well-researched ideas at every level of elected office. Right now, cynical rhetoric and canned rage are drowning out reasonable discourse. We are seeing decision making that is too often bizarrely out of touch with what most of us know to be the realities of everyday life. If you have ideas to offer and solutions that can work, we need your voice in the discussion for the sake of our common future. Right now we

listen to many voices pointing out what is not working and what is never going to work, but the same people are often silent when it comes to offering
solutions—especially to our country's protracted economic emergency. With
growing alarm, we hear more each day of the deepening financial woes and
retrenchments of our states, counties, and school districts. Our elected officials have led us into financial disarray: a condition in which more money is
needed than is had to maintain basic services, infrastructure, and obligations.
They lack workable economic growth strategies to redress the imbalance.

Now is the time to focus on what will move America forward with dignity,
grace, compassion, competence, and accomplishment. Although we will never
reach perfect consensus on how best to move America into a successful and
sustainable future, the fact is that if we don't talk about our ideas, then nothing gets done. Without conversations, debates, and problem-solving discussions, we will not find solutions to our problems. If you feel that your ability
to listen and talk with others is above average, our future depends upon you.
If you believe that debates do not have to make enemies or start wars, our
future depends upon you. If you believe in problem-solving rather than blame-
throwing, our future depends upon you.

America Needs Public Servants, Not Career Politicians

One of the reasons people run for elected office is to become public servants who are focused on public good. During my time in elected office,
when people would confront me about how selfish, high-paid, and uncaring
people in elected office were, my response was that of the 105 legislators
with whom I served, a full 95 to 100 were there as public servants, pursuing
public good. This is not to say that we all agreed on how to fulfill the idea of
"public good," because we didn't. The point is that people were of compas-
sionate heart from their point of view and they were focused on their highest sense of public good rather than being focused on personal gain or personal benefits.

A taunt that I sometimes heard as a candidate was, "Why would you want
to be a politician?" I smiled time after time and said, "I don't. I'm working to
be elected as a public servant." That reply usually brought a smile: "Well,
doesn't it mean the same thing?" Perhaps it has come to mean the same
thing to the general public when thinking about state and federal elected officials, because it has become so hard at these levels to really see public
service in action. However, I invite you and your family members and

friends to look around your communities at all of the elected offices held by people who indeed are serving the public and are in no way acting merely as self-aggrandizing politicians.

It is more important today than ever to distinguish between being a *politician* and being a *public servant*. Being a *politician* implies cultivating a career based on gaining and holding elected office, by engaging in behaviors that are more about money, power, fame, self-service, and getting re-elected than they are about making good and difficult decisions for the greatest good. Being a *public servant* implies working first and foremost to solve problems and accomplish tasks in ways that serve the greatest good for all involved rather than focusing on personal or special-interest gain.

America needs public servants. Every one of our united states, every county, parish, borough, township, city, village, school board, and water board needs public servants rather than politicians in its elected offices. Without public servants to voice the needs of the people, to craft the solutions that will really work in the public interest, and to challenge the policies and lobbies undermining the public interest, America will fail. Only by replacing politicians with genuine public servants can we hope to move toward a bright future.

Our children's lives depend upon us, too. They may not have reached a point in their lives when they might consider running for office. But your knowledge, wisdom, experience, and passionate concern for multigenerational outcomes will enable you to represent their interests by changing things in this country for the better. Without good and capable public servants in elected office, all levels of government suffer and descend further into endless budget woes, union/non-union battles, and splinter-group battles—all driven by anger and us vs. them disputes. These dilemmas and battles leave many bystanders wringing their hands and not knowing what to do.

We don't need more politicians running to serve themselves and their districts only. We need public servants running for office at every level in every election cycle and for every seat so that the good of the whole trumps the gain of the few.

Reasons to Run

I know—just because you are needed doesn't mean you'll necessarily be able and willing to run for elected office. When considering your reason to run, I suggest that you run "for it"—not "to it" and not "despite it." Here's what I mean. Running "for it" means accepting the challenge to run for an office, as opposed to putting on your running shoes and heading out of town. Running "to it" means that you are drawn to the appeal of holding office, like a moth to a flame, with the danger of getting burned once obtained. When I suggest not running "despite it," I mean that you should be motivated by the assurance that you can transform an elected office tarnished by abuse and incompetence into a fit instrument for improving your community and changing your constituents' lives for the better.

Running for office is grueling and invigorating all at the same time. You'll need every ounce of energy you can tap. Knowing all of your reasons for running will help you to maintain your focus and energy. You'll need that thorough self-knowledge to answer the battery of standard questions you'll face from the media and potential contributors and endorsers (more on this in Chapters 7 and 10 through 12).

Over the years, people have asked me why I think people choose to run for elected office. After years of listening and observation, my response is that people choose to run for elected office for many of the same reasons people choose any profession. When I attended the police academy as a cadet, my classmates would give three main reasons why they'd chosen to become police officers: "My dad was a cop;" "I want to serve the community;" and "I want to shoot a gun and drive cars fast—legally." These three reasons boil down to family business, public service, and power.

Sometimes a person chooses a particular career because it's the family business. Think of the professional clustering in families of doctors, scientists, lawyers, veterinarians, police, firefighters, and teachers you know. In the national arena, consider the many political dynasties and successions that have flourished under such family names as Adams, Harrison, Roosevelt, Kennedy, Bush, Gore, Romney, and Clinton. At state and local levels, it is perhaps even more common for certain family names to persist in public office for generations.

Another reason people run for office is public service. Some of us run for office because we believe that holding elected office is a civic duty and responsibility. This is my own credo: "Running for elected office is like being willing to serve on jury duty—if none of us does it, we will throw away the systems of justice and representative government that make us uniquely the United States of America."

Yet another reason people run for office is to aggrandize money, power, and fame. The media focuses on those offices offering the most lucrative rewards to the officeholder. Few elected offices in America, however, pay rich dividends. Indeed, most officeholders forfeit better sources of income in order to perform public service. Admittedly, some power and visibility come with every elected office to some degree, but consider the spectrum. At one end, a precinct worker who is elected precinct committeeperson gets no power with the position—just a lot of work to help a political party. She gets very little visibility—just with the few dozen faithful who typically show up at precinct committee meetings. At the other end of the spectrum, certain state and federal elected officials command global power and attention. Remember that having power is not inherently bad. Leveraging power and visibility to good effect can change the world for the better.

Characteristics of the People We Need in Office

As conscientious citizens, we need to put people in office who are public servants dedicated to making the best possible decisions for the good of the whole, rather than politicians dedicated to serving themselves and their special interests. Public servants need to be vetted for excellence in the following traits, skills, and qualities, all of which are essential to their performing effectively in office: human interaction and management skills, intelligence, knowledge, problem-solving skills, speaking skills, reading skills, listening skills, questioning skills, research skills, backbone, stamina, honesty, decisiveness, empathy, and goal-driven perseverance. Let's look at each of these fifteen performance criteria in turn.

- *Human Interaction and Management Skills*: Human interaction skills are the starting place. You've probably heard the saying, "No one cares about you until they see how much you care about them." This is never truer than when it comes to winning elections. Candidates who relate better to voters (and have more name recognition as a result) often have the upper hand in winning races, even over opponents who are more intelligent, capable, articulate, and skilled. Human interaction skills range from your listening and handshaking skills to your ability to remember names and things about a person from a previous conversation. They also include your ability to lead a team: first your campaign team and then, if elected, your staff. If you as a candidate have a tough time relating to people, you and your campaign team must find a way to overcome this and demonstrate how you will interact with people and do it well. Take customer service, interpersonal relationship, and body-language courses to improve your skill and comfort in interacting with others.

- *Intelligence*: Just because we need intelligent officeholders who can help our world make its way into the future doesn't always mean we elect them. Take for instance, the very nice grandmother who served in the Idaho House when I was there. She was often without a clue on the procedures in motion, the topics under discussion, or the next steps that should be taken. At the same time her ability to connect with people to help them feel they were heard and that their problems would somehow be addressed was a valuable asset. Despite her limited intelligence and precisely because of her constituent care and name recognition, she continues to get re-elected. I continue to maintain that if her constituents really knew that they were not being well-represented, there would be an outcry heard statewide. So, here's what I mean by intelligence: someone can have a high IQ and strong human interaction skills and be a good candidate. However, intelligence is more than just IQ. Today's world needs intelligence in the form of intellectual capabilities, emotional understanding, a nose for research, ability to ask clear questions, and, perhaps most importantly of all, life experience that has provided the foundational intelligence for living effectively and making reasonable decisions. People without these forms of intelligence do get elected and re-elected, so when you vote, ask around to find out whether you are truly being represented well, or whether a really nice person is simply keeping a seat warm and has no aptitude for the job that needs to be done.

- *Knowledge*: An elected official or candidate for elected office does not have to be an expert on all subjects related to the office. What you as an elected official or candidate for elected office do need to be is well-informed about your community, the needs of the people you wish to serve, the realities of the budgets which exist to provide governmental services, and who the go-to people are from whom you will be able to gather relevant, accurate, well-reasoned, and well-documented information, analyses, and briefs. To become well-informed on the subjects related to the office which you hold or are running for requires skilled listening and diligent research. The larger the territory and scope of the position, the more likely you will want a research team to support your information gathering. For instance, you may assign team members to research specific topics, organize town hall meetings so you can hear people's concerns, or research specific areas of concern within your election district.

When contemplating what describes a well-informed person, Patty Collinsworth, writing for *The Christian Science Monitor*, wrote that a well-informed person sees "the world clearly ... not through the cloudy lens of partisanship and prejudice."

- *Problem-Solving Skills*: The American public is tired of blame-throwing, finger pointing, and name calling. Voters disengage when a race is all about bashing other candidates and decrying their policies. Voters expect solutions. Candidates must be able to demonstrate their problem solving skills in action and in laying out cogent ideas for solutions.

- *Speaking Skills*: To be articulate is to be able to speak clearly, to the point, and on topic, and to be easily understood by others. While long, winding, rambling presentations from people who convey how much they care may persuade some people to vote for them, the fact is that America needs people who are both caring and articulate. We've lived through enough rambling and roughshod presentations. It's time for clear solutions and clear plans of action that are good for the present and the future. Take every opportunity to polish your speaking skills. Consider joining Toastmasters.

- *Reading Skills*: To perform effectively as a candidate and elected officeholder, you must bring strong, retentive, and voracious reading skills to the job. You'll read to gather information to respond to phone calls, emails, and letters, to review and approve minutes, to read white papers, to gather news from papers and online stories, to glean information from magazines and trade publications, and to find out what voters are thinking in letters from home. Whether plowing through full-length documents or skimming your staff's digests, reading is a daily part of your job demands.

- *Listening Skills*: Listening, like reading, is also daily part of your job demands. You must be able to hear what people are telling you and asking you on the campaign trail. You must be able to hear people in a variety of settings with a huge difference in noise levels, in the volumes with which people speak, in rooms with poor acoustics, and on audio recordings of variable quality. Listening is the way in which you will gather information that is critical to the decisions you will make. If you have any auditory challenges, get hearing aids or assistive devices. There is truly no way to be effective in committee meetings, council chambers, or on the floors where elected officials meet if you cannot hear or see a transcript of what is being said. Being a strong listener includes being able to understand both content and emotion, both proposals and complaints. Listening is often more important than speaking. Voters want you to listen to them. Talk less; listen more. As an elected official, your success depends on what you hear, listen to, read, and understand.

- *Questioning Skills*: To get the information you want, you need to be able to ask clear questions. You will also need to be able to read listeners' body language so that you know whether they have understood your question. At all times you need to be able to restate your question so that people can understand what you are asking. To restate is to ask the question again using different words; restating a question is not repeating the same words. Questions are your tools for uncovering information, for finding matches or discrepancies, and for discovering what additional questions may still need to be asked and answered before a best-possible decision can be made.

- *Research Skills*: When you don't know something, find out. If you don't know how or where to find out, ask for help. Every community has access to a library, and a research librarian is a great asset. When you think you know the answer, more research may still be helpful. When you do not know the answer, admit it and ask for help.

- *Backbone*: The willingness to stand up, speak up, and stay strong is your public service backbone. We see so much waffling or flip-flopping on positions, failure to commit to a decision and carry it through, and so much unwillingness to even commit to a decision in the first place. Our children know which parent to approach to get their way—the one without backbone. Unless you have backbone, you'll succumb to those who whine and complain. Finding good solutions takes a backseat unless you have backbone. When you have a strong backbone, you ask the right questions, gather the right information, find the right solutions, and implement the right action. Find your backbone now. Unless you have one, the media will catch you in what appear to be conflicting statements or comments. With a backbone, however, you will be trusted as being consistent and forthright, even when people may disagree with your position. To identify where your backbone is, ask yourself: What am I most passionately committed to and most willing to take a stand upon? Until you can answer this question, you are not ready for the candidate questionnaires and the media inquiries that will come your way.

- *Stamina*: Walking four miles in a parade requires stamina. Going door-to-door for eight to twelve hours a day requires physical, emotional, and mental stamina. Standing for two to twelve hours a day in a fair booth requires endurance and stamina. A friend of mine working the fair booth one afternoon said after the first hour of a two-hour shift for volunteers, "How do you do this twelve hours a day, Jana?" I asked in turn, "What do you mean?" She elaborated: "I mean stand here for twelve hours with this sea of humanity, of engagement, of agreement and disagreement, of apathy, of disconnect, and of distraction and still have any energy left?" On the last day of a gun show, at which I had manned my campaign booth for ten hours each day, a neighboring booth owner came over and said: "I don't know how you do it; you listen to experts all weekend telling you what they know and what they think can work and end the weekend with a smile on your face." In both cases I smiled. In the first case, I gave my team volunteer the option to leave if it was simply too exhausting. In the second case, I smiled and said, "I guess I was blessed with the genetics and the personality to survive with a smile." Having stamina is absolutely critical to running a race to win. For some people it is physical stamina that wins. For others it is mental and intellectual stamina that wins. For still others it is the stamina of running year after year with the hope that the physical workload will ease up as one's name recognition spreads. Sleep well. Eat well. Delegate well. You really can't do everything every day and expect yourself to cross the finish line. Start now, get fit enough to walk miles, stand for hours, shake hands by the hundreds, and speak to thousands in one day. Your body must be able to carry you through—the race depends on you.

- *Honesty*: Voters want to know whether you are honest. Every voter will have a different measuring tool to assess your honesty. You know what your own standard for honesty is. Live up to it every day. People can see, hear, and smell honesty. So, establish your personal standard and live up to it. Communicate clearly to your campaign team and staff team members what you expect on the honesty front, and on all fronts. One team member's decision can forever destroy your ratings on the honesty scale. However, you are the only one to manage the daily decisions and choices that can ensure honesty is occurring in all cases, on all days, in all ways.

- *Decisiveness*: The ability to take a firm and unequivocal yes or no stand as befits your principles and judgment is crucial to your effectiveness as a campaigner and elected official. Although a unique trait, decisiveness ties back to having a personal backbone. During my House term, I put on my desk a copy of my book *No! How One Simple Word Can Transform Your Life*, to communicate to my 69 colleagues that I would vote no and was prepared to explain why. Being a pliant yes-person is not representing the people who vote you into office. When you vote no, be prepared to explain your position and offer alternative solutions.

- *Empathy*: A candidate or elected official must care genuinely and passionately for the individual people and communities that he serves or proposes to represent. When people know you care, they will start to care about you as a candidate. Bear in mind, however, that candidates who care with equal passion will care about different things and will have different programs for transforming their care into action. Voters need to understand where you stand and what you care about before they make a decision to vote for you, against you, or for someone else who cares more about what they care about.

- *Perseverance*: There will be moments and possibly even days on end where you may find yourself ready to quit or questioning, "Why am I running?" Don't be a flake. Stick with it. See it through to the end. Learn everything you can. Gather as much information, insight, and intelligence as you can. As soon as you made the commitment to run, people began counting on your reliability. Stay in the race and fight through to its conclusion—win or lose.

You and your team may find that you want to add an additional list of characteristics that are important to you. Whatever your list of personal must-have characteristics includes, be sure that you are clear and committed to living them. Also be sure that your team members are willing to abide by the same standards you expect of yourself.

"Moving Out of the Box *builds on the belief that 2010 and beyond will see a balance of consensus-oriented and command-and-control decision making along with a growing number of commanding collaborators in chief." —* Jana Kemp, *Moving Out of the Box* (2008)

Political Parties and What They Promise Won't Save Us

We see it every election cycle. Promises are made and broken before and after the election. An entire set of encyclopedic volumes could be filled with the promises made by challengers and incumbents. It could be supplemented by another set of volumes showing how the promises were kept, and an even larger set of volumes describing how those promises were broken. Political parties—all of them—make promises to help their candidates stand out from the pack. People in all walks of life make promises based upon what they believe and upon what they hope. Most candidates for office are no different. They make promises based on things they and their party believe and hope. But promises are more than wishes or aspirations. Candidates now and into the future need to stand on their own promises and be able to deliver. Voters are clear that empty promises will not be tolerated—witness the number of people voted out of office for failure to live up to promises.

The world's stage is full of seasoned politicians plodding on with old skills and glib promises. What we sorely need today are leaders who wield collaborative and command-and-control skills with equal dexterity, rather than just one or the other. The 2008 presidential race presented a classic contrast between McCain's command-and-control and Obama's collaborative community-organizing skill sets. What we need from twenty-first century leaders, irrespective of party affiliation, is comprehensive facility in all executive and deliberative modalities of leadership.

The reason political parties can't save us is that they are more focused on themselves and winning elections than they are on the public good. Only individual candidates—from any party or from no party—who are focused on public service can save us. This is why the future depends on you!

Conclusion: Don't Wait for an Open Seat!

While you may determine that your personal timing for a run for office is not now, remember that waiting for an open seat may only make things worse in your community. Life is short. Invest your life in what matters most to you. If running for office is on your heart, in your soul, and an ongoing conversation in your head, now is the time to enter the race. If you are well-informed, connected to what it takes to live life in the twenty-first century, and focused on the greatest good for all concerned, our future depends on you!

Have faith in what you and your voice can contribute to a single office, to the community you wish to serve, to a whole system, and to the world! Keep the faith—jump in to the race that is a fit for you. If you don't, then who will?

The future does depend on you as a voter and as a candidate for elected office. Pinpoint your passion, pick your position, and run!

Pinpoint Your Passion

Passion: A Requirement for Running

You read in Chapter I that people won't care about you until they can see how much you care about them. People also will care about you if they can see that you have passion for a topic, a cause, or a group of people about which they also care. There may be an action that you are passionate about seeing occur in your community, state, or even in our country. If people also want to see that action implemented, then they are more likely to care about you too. Knowing what you are passionate about allows you to tell your personal story and your reason for running in a way that creates interest and generates potential votes.

Some people contemplating a run for office are doing so because they are very clear about their passions. For instance, "I want to change the laws that affect development and construction in my neighborhood." Or, "Drunk driving is not acceptable. My child was killed by a drunk driver and I want to see our laws changed." Another motivation to run for office might be: "Education is the future for our children and our country; I'm getting involved in the process to ensure improvements in education." What are the points of passion driving your run for office?

■ **Note** If your heart is not in the race, you'll lose.

If you don't already know what your passions are, discovering them may take some time. Sharing with listeners and potential voters that you are running again because you already hold office is not enough. Stating that you are from a family that has held elected office and served the public is not enough. Voters are looking for one or more points of connection with you on issues they care passionately about.

Work your way through the following soup-to-nuts list of issues to help identify those you connect with most on a personal level. This is a first step toward zeroing in on the category of office that might make a good match for you. We'll explore the categories of office in some detail in Chapter 3. The list that follows is a only a start. It is arranged alphabetically and coupled with relevant levels of elected office. See where your interests line up:

- *Abortion*: legislature, Congress

- *Agricultural Policy*: legislature, governor, Congress, president

- *Alcohol Control*: council, commission, legislature, Congress

- *Breeding, Livestock, Pets, Animal Control, and Animal Rights*: councils, boards, commissions, legislature, Congress

- *Censorship and Freedom of Speech*: legislature, governor, Congress, president

- *Crime Reduction, Prison Overcrowding, and Mandatory Sentencing*: city, county, legislature, governor, Congress, president

- *Development and Construction Issues*: council, mayor, commission, legislature

- *Dump, Landfill, and Waste Management Issues*: village, township, council, commission, parish

- *Education Issues*: school board, legislature, Congress, state superintendent of education

- *Energy Issues*: councils, commissions, legislature, governor, Congress, president

- *Environmental Issues*: councils, commissions, legislature, governor, Congress, president

- *Equal Rights*: legislature, Congress
- *Fish and Game Issues*: legislature, commission, governor, Congress
- *Free Trade Issues*: Congress
- *Gay Marriage*: legislature, governor, Congress, president
- *Gun Control*: council, commission, legislature, Congress
- *Healthcare*: legislature, governor (because of appointment powers), Congress, president
- *Housing Issues*: council, commission, legislature, Congress
- *Immigration Control*: legislature, governor, Congress, president
- *Juvenile Justice*: judges, magistrates, legislature, governor
- *K-12 and Pre-Kindergarten Education Issues*: school board, legislature, Congress
- *Marine Management Issues*: councils, commissions, marine boards, legislature, Congress
- *Narcotics Control and Legalization*: sheriff, legislature, Congress
- *Parks and Recreation*: township, village, city council, commissions, legislature, Congress
- *Police Policies, Personnel, and Profiling*: township, village, city council government seats
- *Privacy Issues*: some local level offices, but primarily legislature and Congress
- *Quackgrass, Quarterhorses, or Quail*: conservation boards, legislature, Congress
- *Right-of-Way and Eminent Domain*: highway districts, councils, commissions, legislature, Congress
- *Sales Tax*: councils, commissions, legislature
- *Security*: council, commission, legislature, Congress
- *Separation of Church and State*: legislature, governor, Congress, president
- *Sheriff's Powers*: commission, sheriff, legislature, judge
- *Taxes*: council, commission, assessor, legislature, governor, Congress, president

- *Telecommunications*: council, commission, legislature, Congress

- *Terrorism*: governor, Congress, president

- *Texting and Cell Phone Use While Driving*: councils, commissions, legislatures

- *Unionization and Open Shop Rights*: legislature, governor, Congress, president

- *Utilities Regulation*: village, township, council, commission, legislature, governor, Congress, president

- *Veterans Affairs*: legislature, governor, Congress, president

- *Water Rights*: boards, councils, commissions, legislature, land resource commissioners (elected in some states), governor, Congress, president

- *Weed Control*: boards, council, commissions

- *Zoos, Game Parks, and Wildlife Preserves*: village, township, council, commission, special election districts

Spend as much time as you and your team need to expand and refine what issues matter most to you, to be sure that you are running for the right office. Spending this time to identify issues also lays the groundwork for your media responses (Chapters 10 and 11), candidate questionnaire responses, and candidate literature creation (Chapters 7 and 9).

■ **Note** Just because your heart is in the race doesn't mean you'll win.

Passion and Office: Match-Up Quiz

This quiz will help you begin to identify and research categories of elected positions that best match your passions. This is a second look at the positions that may be a match for them. In Chapter 3, we'll discuss each position with enough detail so that you can pick the one for which you will run. At this point, your task is to learn enough about what each elected office position entails so that you can narrow your list of possible positions down to one by the time you finish Chapter 3.

This quiz contains broad questions designed to help you think through the various positions before filing to run for office. It's an important exercise; otherwise you may end up being surprised during the race and feeling like you've signed up for the wrong job.

Think about the people whom you have watched campaign who seemed to be running for the wrong position. I'm reminded of the man who ran for city council saying he was going to "fix education." As passionate and heartfelt as he was, I refused to vote for him. He clearly had no comprehension that a city council position has little to no effect on public school education. He should have been running for the school board instead.

The quiz will also help you test your commitment. Sometimes, for example, people get talked into running to represent the party in a race. Once into the campaign, they begin to realize just how much work is involved. That's why, during campaigns every year, there are candidates who drop out because they've discovered just how much time it takes, how much personal pressure they must withstand, and how much they feel burdened by the expectations of others.

Spend enough time on the questions that follow to be sure you can say "Yes, I have a good sense of what this job will require and I'm willing to run anyway." Respond to each of the questions with your first reaction. Circle your "YES" or "NO" answer and move to the next question quickly. We are sorting out what you are most drawn to and therefore what position you are most likely to stay committed to, beginning to end.

1. *Level of Service:*

   a. I care most about my immediate local community and things like dogs barking, land development, sewers, water-use, soil conservation, and my child's school situation.
   YES NO

   b. I care most about the well-being of my state and such areas as business law, agricultural law, educational leadership for the state, taxes, and the future of our state.
   YES NO

   c. I care most about the well-being of this country and such areas as upholding the U.S. Constitution, foreign policy, military protection, our economic standing in the world, taxes, interstate commerce, and supporting research that will keep America innovating for the next one hundred years.
   YES NO

2. *Arena of Interest:*

   a. I am most interested in making rules, policies, and laws that will make our community, state, or country a better place to live.
   YES NO

   b. I am most interested in leading discussions; signing bills into law; implementing laws, rules, and policies; or heading governmental agencies or departments.
   YES NO

   c. I am most interested in enforcing laws and making rulings on whether laws have been followed or broken.
   YES NO

3. *Arena of Concern:*

   a. I care most about discussing and effecting policies in my local area.
   YES NO

   b. I care most about discussing and effecting policies happening in and around my state.
   YES NO

   c. I care most about discussing and effecting policies happening around the U.S. and around the world.
   YES NO

4. *Length of Service:*

   a. I am most inclined to run for a two-year position.
   YES NO

   b. I am most inclined to run for a four-year position.
   YES NO

   c. I am most inclined to run for a six-year position.
   YES NO

5. *Party Affiliation:*

   a. I prefer to keep my political party affiliation to myself.
   YES NO

   b. I am happy to announce my political party affiliation and to run as a party candidate.
   YES NO

   c. I am convinced the political party system is not working and will declare to run as an independent candidate.
   YES NO

6.   *My Skills:*

    a.   Listening, responding to phone calls, responding to letters and emails, hearing different points of view before commenting on my own.
YES   NO

    b.   Speaking, debating, serving on panels, responding to questions in person.
YES   NO

    c.   Solving problems, offering ideas and options while seeking and finding solutions, and following up to see what has happened.
YES   NO

    d.   Fundraising, asking for money, attending events to ask for money, making phone calls to ask for money, sending letters and emails to ask for money, asking for money from everyone I know and meet.
YES   NO

    e.   All of the above.
YES   NO

Analyze Your Answers

First, count your NO responses. How many do you have? If you have more than ten NO answers, it may be time to reconsider whether you are passionate enough to run for office and win.

Now, count your YES responses. How many do you have? If you have more than ten YES answers, read on to discover which positions you have begun to pinpoint as potential fits.

The *office-matching implications of YES answers* are given below:

1.   *Level of Service:*

    a.   I care most about my immediate, local community and things like dogs barking, land development, sewers, water-use, soil conservation, and my child's school situation.
YES: Then you'll want to run for offices such as seats on boards, councils, and commissions in local districts, villages, townships, cities, counties/boroughs/parishes/districts, and local trade associations or civic groups. You might also consider leadership positions like supervisor, mayor, chief, etc.

b. I care most about the well-being of my state and such areas as business law, agricultural law, educational leadership for the state, taxes, and the future of our state.
   YES: Then you'll run for such offices as assemblyperson, council-person, senator or representative at any of the following levels: district/ state, state, and possibly state/federal offices. Elected positions at these levels also include judge, auditor, state's attorney, etc.

c. I care most about the well-being of this country and such areas as upholding the U.S. Constitution, foreign policy, military protection, our economic standing in the world, taxes, interstate commerce, and supporting research that will keep America innovating for the next one hundred years.
   YES: Then you'll run for such offices as U.S. senator or member of Congress, president, and vice president. Or, you'll pursue international involvement in civic groups and trade associations by election or appointment. You may also choose to pursue an appointment at any level of service as a way to prepare yourself for elected office.

2. *Arena of Interest:*

   a. I am most interested in making rules, policies, and laws that will make our community, state, or country a better place to live.
      YES: Legislative branch offices, such as council, commission, legislative, or congressional seats, are the elected offices to pursue.

   b. I am most interested in leading discussions, signing bills into law, implementing laws, rules, and policies, or heading governmental agencies or departments.
      YES: Executive branch offices such as mayor, county commissioner, governor, secretary of state, controller, county treasurer, county assessor, county clerk, auditor general, lieutenant governor, superintendent of education (and the corresponding titles in your state).

   c. I am most interested in enforcing laws and making rulings on whether laws have been followed or broken.
      YES: Executive or judicial branch offices such as sheriff, state attorney general, district attorney, coroner, medical examiner, magistrate and other elected judgeships. Note: Judgeships in many states or category are by appointment only.

3. *Arena of Concern:*

    a. I care most about discussing and effecting policies in my lo-
        cal area.
        *YES: Council, assembly, commission, mayor, sheriff, and legisla-
        tive seats are the elected offices to pursue.*
    b. I care most about discussing and effecting policies in and
        around my state.
        *YES: Commission legislative and gubernatorial seats are the
        elected offices to pursue.*
    c. I care most about discussing and effecting policies in the
        U.S. and around the world.
        *YES: Congress, some legislative and all state and federal execu-
        tive offices.*

4. *Length of Service:*

    a. I am most inclined to run for a two-year position.
        *YES: Some council and commission seats, state house and senate
        seats, U.S. House seats.*
    b. I am most inclined to run for a four-year position.
        *YES: Council, commission, sheriff, governor, lieutenant governor,
        controller, treasurer, auditor, state superintendent of instruction/
        education, and the corresponding offices in your state. President
        and Vice-President of the U.S.*
    c. I am most inclined to run for a six-year position.
        YES: U.S. Senate and some judgeships.

5. *Party Affiliation:*

    a. I prefer to keep my political party affiliation to myself.
        *YES: In most states, the non-partisan offices are sheriff and
        council positions. Some commission positions, but not all are non-
        partisan. Judgeships and the Nebraska legislature, by law, are
        always non-partisan.*
    b. I am happy to announce my political party affiliation and to
        run as a party candidate.
        *YES: Some commission positions. State-level house, senate, and
        executive branch offices. U.S. House and Senate seats. President
        and Vice-President of the U.S.*
    c. I am convinced the political party system is not working and
        will declare to run as an independent candidate.
        *YES: Most states allow independent candidates in every race.
        However, the rules for an independent to get on the ballot*

> *are different in every state. More on getting on the ballot in Chapter 5.*

6. *My Skills:*

    a. All of the above is the best answer here. However, the reality is that not all of us are good at all of the skills needed for success. My biggest personal skill gap: fundraising. What is your biggest skill gap? Once you've identified it/them, then find campaign team members who can help you succeed in the skill sets you personally do not have well-covered yourself.

What have you learned? Is the position you first thought you'd run for still the best match for your passion and interests? What position(s) are you now focused on learning more about?

Choose a Starting Position

Many party faithful will tell you to start small and work your way up to represent ever bigger districts. In some cases this is good advice, in others it is simply posturing to keep you as a candidate from interfering with other party-endorsed candidates. Or, they'll suggest you pay your dues first by holding elected offices within the party so that you can earn the right (in their eyes) to run for a public office. Dirk Kempthorne's career to date provides a good example of stepwise advancement, perhaps toward the ultimate goal of the U.S. presidency: University of Idaho Student Body President, Mayor of Boise, U.S. Senator from Idaho, Governor of Idaho, and most recently U.S. Secretary of the Interior, appointed by President George W. Bush. Whichever strategy you pursue—starting small and working your way up, or starting with the office you really want—be clear with yourself about your objective, because you will be asked continually, "Why are you running?"

Choose a Position You'll Enjoy

Enjoyment is not a luxury when running for office; it's a necessity. Even if your primary motivation for running is discontent or anger—such as "drunk-driving laws need changing," or "no more dairy barns can go up in our community," or "no more wars"—you'll need to tap sources of your joy to function effectively.

For example, working to improve the lives of children is a noble passion. If you truly care about kids and their well-being and want to work on early childhood education, foster-care situations, higher education, child health-care, and all of the items related to the life and legal well-being of children, then a position on the school board or state legislature is likely something you'll enjoy. However, if you don't care about improving the lives of children, then don't run for the school board. You'll be miserable. If you're running for an office like state representative, don't tell voters your passion is kids and don't make child-related issues part of your platform. Voters can smell liars a mile away.

The length of a position's term may be a factor in your enjoyment. For instance, if you know that you are more of a start-up entrepreneurial type, then a six-year senate term may seem like a lifetime sentence, whereas a two- or four-year position at any level may seem more tolerable. On the other hand, if you are a maintainer, who likes to work on projects for years and decades, then serving multiple six-year terms in a position may be the match for you.

The people with whom you surround yourself will also influence your level of joy in running for office. Choose team members who share your vision, passion, and approach to problem-solving. You'll need team members who can get work done and who "keep the faith" when times are tough.

When choosing the elected office position for which you most want to run, ask someone already holding the position two simple questions: "Why do you keep running? What is it that you most enjoy about this work?" Interviewing people who hold the position you are considering will help you refine why you want the job. Whatever position you select, be sure that you will have moments of enjoyment along the way. Without joy, it is difficult to maintain your energy and passion, which makes it difficult to maintain your stamina.

How's Your Stamina?

We touched on this critical question in the preceding chapter. Without the stamina and endurance to run and complete your race, and then serve in office once you win, you will find yourself suffering. Your family and friends will be frustrated with and worried about you and your health.

One brilliant attorney friend and mentor who ran for U.S. Senate said to me during my race for governor: "This may leave you alone, naked, and without family or friends when it is over." What he meant by naked was that the gloves will come off during many races and people will say things that are both true and not true. People will dig for and find problematic information in your past that may be so old you've forgotten about it, and people will try to tear you down so much that you feel naked, even when you are fully clothed. What he meant by alone is, sadly, what happens frequently when one campaigns for an office: divorce. I'm happy to report that my life is intact, with no sense at all of having been stripped naked, and with my husband, family, and friendships still very much in place. Yes, there certainly were days when I felt frustrated and exhausted—just ask my treasurer.

There are plenty of resources to tap to discover what you personally need to do every day to be fit, to protect your health, and to stay mentally on top of your game. For starters, answer these questions for yourself, then share your answers with your family and campaign team.

- *How much sleep do I need?* If you don't get your right amount of sleep, it will begin to show. In a world driven by media, you want to look and feel your best every day.

- *What foods do I prefer?* What foods am I allergic to? What foods would I prefer not to eat? Have someone on your team know this so that he or she can work with event planners to meet your needs. It is not a good idea for you to appear picky when you simply have dietary needs that a group should be willing to address. Then there are practical issues of image: I love broccoli, but because my teeth collect broccoli, I avoid eating broccoli in public.

- *What beverages will I drink?* Drink lots of water. Stay hydrated because you will be so busy that it will be easy to become dehydrated in any weather. If you get tipsy quickly from alcohol, don't drink it. Let me repeat: don't drink it. Consider what effect beverages have on you and your ability to speak or answer questions. Also consider what perceptions others have about you depending on what you drink. Running for office is about you and about how you manage people's perceptions of you. My life-long decision has been not to drink alcohol; so, as a candidate for office, I was even careful to put water glasses (which can look like wine glasses) down or to move them out of the picture frame. My lifelong belief about what people drink is this: as long as people drink alcohol responsibly, I don't take issue with what they drink. Which brings us to ...

- *What beverages will I allow my campaign to serve?* Serving alcohol brings legal liabilities into the mix. So, review carefully with your team, your lawyer, and your event hosts what you expect on the beverage front. During my campaigns, I never allowed the campaign to purchase alcohol. Never. You must make your own decision about how to best handle this decision.

- *What exercise routine will I follow?* How much time will you need in your daily and weekly schedule to achieve your personal exercise requirements?

- *Who will drive the car?* This is a serious stamina-related question. You want a driver you can trust. You want a driver who keeps the gas tank full. You want a driver who knows how to get anywhere, or how to follow directions to anywhere, so that you do not have to be the copilot. You want a driver who will talk when you want to and be silent when you need silence. You are the candidate.

- *What shoes will I wear?* More important than you think! Shoes affect your posture and your energy levels. You'll be standing a lot, maybe even more than you ever have in your life. You'll be standing in dirt, on asphalt, on carpet, on concrete. You'll be walking in sand, in dirt, on asphalt, on concrete, on grass, in the rain, in the snow, in the heat, and in every environment you have in your community and state. Wear the pair of shoes or boots you find most comfortable. Keep your shoes and boots shined; military and law enforcement people recognize and respect shined shoes from miles away. Keep your shoes in repair and have a great shoe repair person on call. Have a second pair of your favorite shoes at the ready wherever you go. A whole essay could be written about how important shoes are to your campaign. Shoes are equally important to male and female candidates.

- *How will I shake hands?* No, I'm not kidding. How you manage the act of shaking hands will affect your health. Maybe you've heard the stories of people who are running for office and always have hand-sanitizer products available. Candidates do this to stay healthy. Maybe you've seen candidates with arms in slings? The business of meeting people includes shaking hands, and if you haven't mastered safe handshaking, you can literally get hurt. Practice shaking hands with people you know so that you get the hang of just how tightly, how long, and how many up and down movements you will engage in before you let go of someone's hand. In fact, the book *Primary Colors* has a great discussion of all the ways a candidate can shake hands and what each handshake means. Have a campaign person research the handshakes for you. My handshaking stories include these three: (1) Before one county fair event, my right wrist and hand were feeling tired, so I opted to wear a $15 wrist/hand brace that signaled to people, "go easy on the handshake." It worked because by the end of the fair my wrist and hand had actually recovered.

(2) "My, you have a firm handshake!" is a phrase I heard more than once, and sometimes it was a impressive surprise to the person I was meeting. You will want to determine your own style of shaking hands so that you both stay healthy and make a good impression on others. (3) A male candidate, my same age, who was running for his first U.S. Congressional term, shook my hand as though I was his 110-year-old grandmother. I found the handshake to be offensive, so much so that I mentioned it to one of his campaign team members. Sure enough, the next time I shook his hand, it was the professional peer handshake that I had expected in the first place.

If these paragraphs seem obvious to you, terrific. You are ready to run for office. If the above paragraphs are surprises and yet you are ready to tackle them, you are ready to run. If the above paragraphs seem to involve too many things to manage, it may be time to ask yourself how serious you are about running. No matter how this stamina discussion strikes you, it is once again time to ask yourself, "Why am I really running?"

Why Are You Really Running?

Have you answered that question convincingly for yourself? Now is the time to be brutally honest. If you are not clear about your motivation for running, the media and the public will eat you alive or crush you. You won't be clear with your answer, or it will sound like you are working a hidden agenda. Either way, you're done. Some days you may be asked three hundred times, "Why are you running?" The last time you respond, at 11:00 p.m., must be just as passionate as your first response of the day was at 7:00 a.m.

Again, this is the time to be honest with yourself. We're talking about you and your reason for running. Not your spouse's reason, not your kid's reason, not that it is your civic duty. Why are YOU really running?

Candidates say they are running for office for any number of reasons:

- *I can do the job better than the people in office.* While this may be true, how can you convince voters to support you and your ability to do the job? You'll need to have an action you are committed to, a law you want to change, or an issue that you will champion before people will start to engage with you.

- *I can't stand by any longer. It is time to get involved and save our community (or state, or country)!* This is a good start. However, what are you specifically going to do to "save" us? Many people are dissatisfied with how things are, too. However, they'll expect to hear from you what you plan to do to make a difference. Better to be specific: "I'm getting involved to save our community from the senseless development that is putting neighborhoods, schools and parks in conflict with liquor stores, shopping malls, and agricultural mega-projects." With specifics, people can picture what you are telling them and decide on the spot whether they agree and want to help you get into office.

- *My child was hit by a drunk driver and I want drunk drivers off the road.* This life experience has been the reason many people have run for office and won. Being focused on one issue so clearly and passionately creates a positively contagious vision that other people can relate to and can decide to support.

- *Our businesses are suffering and lawmakers are passing laws that stand in our way of being successful.* This is a good start, but you'll need to have specific examples of where business is being hurt, what the problem laws are, and how you'll do a better job representing, advocating, and creating legislation favorable to businesses.

- *Because* ... (saying because and looking away, or saying because and pausing too long loses your listeners.) Know why you want to run and have it roll right off your tongue every time you are asked the why question.

- *Because I've paid my dues in the party system and it's my turn to run.* While this feeling may be real and you really do feel it is your turn, voters don't care about this. The only people who care about this reasoning are the handful of political party people who are playing this game too. I repeat, the majority of voters don't care.

- *Because I've got an issue that I want people to hear about.* Consider my Idaho colleague Mr. Marvin Richardson, who has legally changed his name to "Pro-Life." Mr. Pro-Life is so genuinely passionate about bringing an end to abortions, about organic farming, and about bringing an end to unjustified wars that he felt changing his name was the best way to keep his discussion points in front of people. Each election cycle, Mr. Pro-Life runs for Congress or for governor. What is your issue?

- *Because I want to improve the ... by ...* This phrasing shows what you care about, that you are a problem solver, and what action you plan to take.

- *It seems like the right thing to do.* This is a weak response. Again, you may genuinely feel this way. However, it is not a response that prompts voters to keep listening to you. Sentences as short and simple as this can kill your campaign before you even get started.

Here are sound ways to preface your statement of reasons for running:

- "I am running for office because … [state your passionate concerns]"

- "I am running for office to … [state what your passionate action items]"

- "I am running for office because the person in office now needs to go and I plan to … [state your platform's lead points]"

Whatever your real reason for running, you need to become so clear about it that you can smoothly and convincingly answer the question with passion every time you are asked, "Why are you running?" Even on the days you are tired and questioning yourself why you are running, you must consistently and cogently declare your reasons. Remember that no one but you, your family, and a few members of your campaign team need to know that you are having doubts. Yes, these days are going to happen because the process of running most races is so intense, challenging, and time consuming. Recall from Chapter 1 the three fundamental reasons people seek any job, including elected office: family tradition, public service, and money or power. Voters will want to know why you are in the race, and they'll be able to tell which of these three reasons is your real reason for running.

Conclusion

Spend some time now writing down your passionate reasons for a run for elected office. Write a paragraph or list articulating and ranking your reasons. Have at least three people read and discuss it so that you can gather input on what others think and feel about the clarity and strength of your reasons for running the race and holding office.

What you describe now as your passion for running is what will sustain you through the entire race. Be clear about why you are running. You'll have to repeat your reason for running day after day.

We need passionate people to run for office. Without passion, you are unlikely to find the energy, drive, and stamina to run the race and win. Pinpoint your passion so you can pick the position for which you really want to run.

Pick the Position

You can't just assume a political position. That's a good thing. You will benefit most from picking your position as a result of careful research and of carefully building a knowledge base that proves you know what you are talking about. The position for which you are announcing a campaign must be the right match for you, your skills, and your knowledge.

In Chapter 2, you discovered that your passions have led you to several possible positions. In this chapter, you'll work on narrowing the list of positions to the one office for which you want to run and to conduct a campaign to win. If you are thinking, "I've already decided on the office," read this chapter anyway to make sure you have really decided on the best match for who you are and what you want to do.

At the very least, read this chapter so that when you are running for or holding an office you will know what duties make up each position. Suppose you're running for the state legislature and someone asks you about the dump owned by the county. You can reply without missing a beat: "You'll want to talk to the county commissioners about your concerns for the dump. That's outside of the scope of the position I'm running for. I'm running for the state house of representatives because [of reasons X, Y, and Z], and I'm asking for your vote." This scenario actually happened to me while out campaigning door-to-door. All constituents have concerns they want to express, and they want those concerns to be heard and addressed. When you are clear about where those concerns can best be addressed, you can help inform voters whom to contact to get their concerns heard and re-solved. You can at the same time reinforce the concerns that do fit within your area of influence. You can demonstrate that you have the necessary solicitude and knowledge to do the job.

What to Expect When Running for or Holding Elected Office

Even the best job is not always an unadulterated joy. When running for and holding elected office, you will discover that the work has many aspects as the carousel turns: the good, the neutral, the not-so-good, and the downright ugly.

The Good Aspects

- *You'll meet new people and learn new things every day.* If this doesn't sound to you like a truly excellent aspect of the job, you'd better reconsider whether you should be running for office at all. Meeting as many people as you can and asking them for their vote is now a part of your daily work assignment. You'll also be learning constantly and in whatever degree of detail you choose all about the people, issues, concerns, and opportunities in your community, district, state, and country.

- *You'll receive lots of attention.* Many people will be paying attention to you because, if elected, you will be empowered to make and influence decisions that affect their everyday lives. Many people will be willing to provide you with information, some of which will be helpful and some of which may be useless or worse. Also, beware of accepting gifts or privileges from people: some people will want to give you things that you cannot accept because campaign law prevents you from doing so. Consult your local and state election offices to learn about the laws affecting your race.

- *You'll get invited to many meetings and events.* This will be good for gathering information and building networks.

- *You will be respected.* Contrary to popular belief, almost everyone respects a person who runs for office. Running for office takes personal resolve and moral courage, and most people admire such proof of character regardless of partisan differences.

- *You win the seat you are seeking and can make a positive difference in the world.*

The Neutral Aspects

- *You will be approached any time about any topic.* Staying alert, receptive, and neutral about your public availability will prevent you from responding in a way that alienates you from the very people with whom you are working to connect.

- *Not everyone will agree with you.* Treat this as a neutral point so that you don't find yourself in an argument you can never win but which make you look prickly and disagreeable.

- *You may win the race and you may lose the race.* Of course, you may be among the one percent who enter a race not to win but to make a point. Even if you are among the other ninety-nine, treat winning and losing as a neutral item so that your desire to win doesn't outweigh your desire to do what is right and dignified. You will live to run another day—if that's what you want.

The Not-So-Good Aspects

- *Know that your family members may be asked by others what you think.* This may not be good for your campaign because family members do not always know what you would say. Family members should not be put in the hot seat of speaking on your behalf unless they are fully prepared to speak for you and the campaign. Some families agree that family members should be able to answer questions. Other families agree that the best answer is, "I am not the candidate. You'll want to ask the candidate."

- *You'll get invited to more meetings than you can possibly attend.* This is also challenging, because your time with family and friends can become nonexistent and you can only ingest so much information before hitting saturation.

- *You'll receive conflicting information and have to sort out what is true, right, and best.* You'll have so much information coming toward you on one day that it is overwhelming. For instance, hot-button issues will prompt people to send you untold volumes of data and stories. On another day you won't be able to get your hands on the information that seems like it should exist in an easy-to-find location. For instance, while in office I searched for data on what percent of a First World country's population could be realistically sustained as welfare recipients and I could not find any data to answer this question.

- *You'll discover that voters don't know who the current officeholder is or what the official does.* You have to spend time educating voters about things not related to you and your campaign. Stay polite—you may win their votes anyway.

- *You win the seat you are seeking and discover that you can't make the positive difference you had hoped to make, or that you can't make it in what seems like a reasonable amount of time to you.*

The Downright Ugly

- *People expect you to be available 24/7.* They expect you to always care deeply about their issues and concerns.

- *You'll receive phone calls, email messages, and letters that contain lies, insults, or anonymous threats.* You'll also read blogs, chatroom posts, and tweets spreading lies about your positions or yourself, scurrilous language, and occasionally, threats.

- *The children at your child's school may be mean and ugly toward your child and you.*

- *You can expect name-calling from your opponent's camp in person, in print, and in advertisements.* Decide how you and your team will run your campaign. No one has to head in this direction. I say it is time for leaders to emerge in every race: true leaders do not name-call or bully. True leaders ask questions about facts and make opinions known without name-calling. More on this in Chapter 6.

- *You will become downright ugly if you don't take care of yourself and maintain your stamina.* This is no joking matter. You'll be crabby and short-tempered. You'll find yourself without patience or energy for the people you love. You may look exhausted when photographed. That leads voters to wonder how you'll hold up once you have the job. Take care of yourself.

- *Safety must be monitored at all times.* High-profile candidates and officeholders in the federal, executive, and legislative branches are provided with security detail at public expense. By and large, candidates and officeholders at other levels of government are not protected in this way. Yet our safety is also put in jeopardy just because we choose to run for office. When I ran for the Idaho House, my biggest safety concern was the possibility of being attacked by dogs while I was campaigning door-to-door. When I ran for Idaho governor, my biggest safety concern was for my life and the lives of my family. During my 2010 gubernatorial run, I filed three police reports: the first with the Idaho State Police in order to protect myself from people in the Idaho corrections system; the second with my city police department to procure a restraining order against someone threatening my family members; and the third with a federal office of law enforcement to provide them with information regarding a credible threat to my physical safety. No matter where you are, you and your team should be aware of safety factors, how to exit the scene safely, and how to get into an unmarked vehicle to be driven away from the scene. The mass shooting of U.S. Representative Gabrielle Giffords and eighteen others at a community event she was hosting in 2011 is a recent reminder of the omnipresent danger that attends elective office and the need to have a safety plan to protect yourself, your family, and your campaign team members.

What Position Will You Pursue?

Whether your aim is to be elected the president of the United States or a member of your local school board, it is incumbent upon you to learn about the whole spectrum of other offices that might complement, constrain, or otherwise interact with your own. Getting to know those pertinent offices, their responsibilities, and the people in them is a prerequisite to your success in office. Knowing whom to talk to and how they can help is crucial to your building the collaborative resource base you'll need to solve problems for the good of your nation, state, and community.

Let's revisit the Chapter 2 quiz and look in more detail at what each level and type of elected office involves. The following descriptions will not only help you to decide which office you want pursue; they will also help you to orient yourself within the ecology of other offices among which your chosen office operates. The various types of elective bodies and offices are considered under the following levels: local, district and state, and federal. They are then briefly considered by branch (legislative, executive, or judicial) and area of interest.

Local Positions

- *Neighborhood Boards*: Running for a homeowners' association board counts as running for elected office. You'll have to campaign. You'll have regular meetings, homework, budgets, contracts, and impromptu meetings. You'll have problems to solve. You'll be managing tough interactions—neighbors in debate and even fights.

- *School Organizations*: You'll have to campaign for positions on the school board, PTO, PTA, or other school groups. You'll have regular meetings, homework, and impromptu meetings. You'll have problems to solve.

- *Local District Boards*: Water board, co-op board, soil district, highway district, auditorium district, water district, conservation district— each of these geographically and domain-specific districts is responsible for setting and implementing rules, ordinances, policies, fee-setting, fee collection, decision-making meetings, management and oversight of resources, and personnel management. Check with your county/parish elections clerk to find out about all of the possibilities of running for local board positions.

- *Village, Township, and City Councils*: Each of these councils is responsible for setting and implementing ordinances, policies, fee-setting, fee collection, decision-making meetings, management and oversight of resources, and personnel management. Check with your village, town, or city offices to confirm what positions are available.

- *Mayor*: Whether part-time or full-time, a mayor has leadership and management responsibilities tied to the council, staff, municipal workers, contractors, and police, as well as to budgets, management of resources, addressing constituent concerns, and planning and zoning responsibilities. Additionally, some cities have parks, zoos, and other community centers to manage.

- *County/Borough/Parish Commissioners*: Whether part-time or full-time, commissioners have partnership responsibilities related to other county-elected officials such as a county treasurer, sheriff, county assessor, county coroner. Commissioners usually have leadership and management responsibilities for all of the departments within the county. They also have planning and zoning responsibilities. The responsibilities include personnel and budget items.

- *Trade and Professional Associations, Unions, and Civic Groups*: Although these are non-governmental organizations, many do hold elections for boards from among their memberships. Many of these organizations invest in community-building projects that bring value and often save governmental organizations money and human resource investments.

District and State Positions

- *Commissioner (County/District):* See above.

- *Sheriff (County):* You will oversee deputies, jails, budgets, and civilian personnel, provide leadership on community safety needs, and exercise unique law enforcement powers. Study all relevant constitutions, laws, and ordinances to be sure you are ready for what this job entails.

- *Assessor (County):* You will determine the value of property and buildings, set tax levy amounts, collect property taxes, and work closely with county commissioners on budgets.

- *District Attorney (City/County):* Not all jurisdictions hold elections for this position. In some cases, a local body of officials appoints the district attorney. The D.A.'s duties are to defend the city or county in lawsuits and to prosecute alleged criminals in the jurisdiction. You need to be a practicing and bar-registered attorney in your state to be eligible for to run for this position.

- *Coroner or Medical Examiner (County/District):* You will determine cause of death, give reports to law enforcement, and testify in trials as needed. You do not necessarily have to be a medical doctor to hold this position. Check with your election office.

- *Judge or Magistrate (County/District/State):* You will interpret the law, preside over court hearings and trials, rule on court cases, and write judicial opinions.

- *College Board (District/State):* Some districts and states have community college boards with elected members. These boards are responsible for educational standards, accreditation, budgets, personnel, student standards, and sometimes course planning.

- *School Board (District/State):* Nearly every school district has a board with three to seven members. Some schools also have elected governing boards. In general, school boards oversee the K-12 school(s) in their district. Responsibilities include educational standards, student policies, teacher contracts, staff contracts, building and grounds, athletics, budgets, and every aspect of managing and operating a school. Many states have state boards of education, variously filled by election and by gubernatorial appointment.

- *Auditorium Board (District/State):* Some states have convention center or auditorium boards that oversee sports facilities, parks, and meeting facilities. These elections are often obscure, yet these boards have a big impact on a district-wide and state-wide economy.

- *Water, Soil, Water, Conservation, or Marine Board (District/State):* You will be responsible for managing resources, budgets, and personnel tied to your respective area of jurisdiction and expertise.

- *Legislator (County/State):* Your primary responsibility will be to review, debate, modify, and enact laws on every subject imaginable, including budgets.

- *Governor (State):* You will provide your state with vision and leadership, represent your state vis-à-vis other states and the federal government, and implement the laws, rules, and policies established by the state legislature. You will make legislative and budget proposals to the state legislature; lead and manage your state's human, financial and natural resources; and make appointments to thousands of seats on state boards, commissions, task forces, and councils each year. You will be the commander-in-chief of the National Guard in your state. You will sign legislation into law and exercise veto power.

- *Lieutenant Governor:* Your chief responsibilities will be to support the state senate and to serve in lieu of the governor during the governor's absence or incapacity. This position is sometimes used as a stepping stone to run for governor.

- *State Auditor, Controller, and Treasurer:* Each position has different responsibilities tied to the monies of the state, and can include auditing, managing monies, paying bills and payroll, and implementing state financial policies.

- *Secretary of State:* You will manage personnel, budget, and business filings, oversee elections, and implement laws and policies related to business and elections.

- *State Superintendent of Education:* You will be responsible for state educational policy, budget, and personnel management affecting public schools in your state, including K-12 and often post-secondary schools. You will be called upon to testify before the legislature; to provide vision for adapting public instruction to economic, technological, and social changes; to comply with federal legislation respecting standards, funding eligibility, and mandates; and to balance and accommodate the needs of students, teachers, and other employees of public schools and the department of education with the public interest.

- *State Attorney General*: You will represent the state in lawsuits and all legal matters. You will manage your department's staff, budget, and litigation calendar; research and interpret the U.S. Constitution and state constitution, precedents, and applicable laws and facts; assess and decide legal agenda; and issue legal opinions.

Federal Positions

- *U.S. Senator or Representative*: U.S. senators and representatives are variously responsible for representing the interests of their states and electorates on the federal level, reviewing, amending, and enacting federal legislation, establishing budgets, declaring war, and providing checks and balances upon each other and the executive, judicial, and regulatory branches of government.

- *U.S. President*: You will be the commander-in-chief of all U.S. military branches; sign or veto all federal legislation; shape and implement legislation and national and international policies in all areas; make thousands of cabinet, staff, departmental, agency, military, ambassadorial, judicial, and other appointments each year; and serve as the leader, personification, and spokesperson of the United States of America at home and abroad.

- *U.S. Vice President*: You will support the president as directed by the latter; serve as president of the Senate; assume presidential powers in the president's absence; and succeed the president in the event of the latter's incapacity or death.

Branch

Is your public service interest most closely tied to the legislative, executive, or judicial branch of government? The following descriptors can help you refine the position you'd most like to pursue.

Legislative: I am most interested in making rules, policies, and laws that will make our community, state, or country a better place to live. Examples:

- city councilor

- commissioner (all levels of government)

- county, state, federal, territorial, or commonwealth legislator

Executive: I am most interested in leading discussions, signing laws, and implementing laws, rules, and policies as the head of a governmental agency or department. Examples:

- mayor
- commissioner (all levels of government)
- governor
- secretary of state
- controller, auditor general, or treasurer
- lieutenant governor
- superintendent of education

Judicial: I am most interested in enforcing laws and making rulings on whether laws have been followed or broken. Examples:

- sheriff
- district attorney
- coroner or medical examiner
- attorney general
- elected judge or magistrate

Area of Interest

Local: I care most about discussing and effecting issues in my local area. Possible matches:

- councilor
- mayor
- commissioner
- sheriff
- legislator

State: I care most about discussing and effecting issues happening in and around my state. Possible matches:

- commissioner
- legislator

- governor

National and International: I care most about discussing and effecting issues happening around the U.S. and around the world. Possible matches:

- U.S. senator or representative
- All federal executive officers

Education: Possible matches:

- PTA/PTO president
- school board member
- state legislator
- state superintendent of education or instruction
- U.S. senator or representative

Transportation: Possible matches:

- highway district or commissioner
- county or parish commissioner
- state legislator
- U.S. senator or representative

Business: Possible matches:

- state legislator
- secretary of state
- U.S. senator or representative

Children and Families: Possible matches:

- commissioner
- school board member
- state legislator
- U.S. senator or representative

Agriculture: Possible matches:

- soil, water and conservation district member
- state legislator

- U.S. senator or representative

Taxes. Possible matches:

- city councilor
- county commissioner
- county assessor
- state legislator
- governor
- U.S. senator or representative
- U.S. president

Constitution: Possible matches:

- magistrate
- judge
- state legislator
- governor
- U.S. senator or representative
- U.S. president

Environment: Possible matches:

- soil & conservation district board member
- water district board member
- marine district board member
- city council
- county commissioner
- state legislator
- U.S. senator or representative

Revisit the list of alphabetized topics in Chapter 2 and your own list to determine whether you are zeroing in on the elected offices that most closely match your interests and qualifications. Other issues you should consider are length of service (treated elsewhere in this chapter) and party affiliation (treated in Chapter 5).

Ensure the Position Is a Good Fit for Your Passion and Skills

Do you have the right skills and credentials for the position you are seeking? Every elected position requires some subset of the skills reviewed in Chapters 1 and 2. Some elected positions—such as sheriff, judge, attorney general, and sometimes coroner—require accredited expert skills and professional accreditation. Consult your county election clerk or secretary of state to learn the prerequisites you must meet to be eligible to file to run for any particular office.

Here is another round of considerations for your review. Here's a look at the activities and schedules of people in office.

- *Part-time positions*: You'll discover that almost every elected office that is classified as part-time is, done properly, a full-time job. This is certainly the case for such responsible part-time positions as mayor, county clerk, and even lieutenant governor. It is also the case for other part-time elected positions on boards, city councils, county/ parish commissions, and in legislatures and nongovernmental organizations. Such positions are often unpaid or nominally paid, yet they require incessant homework, meetings, events, research, and constituent conversations throughout the day, week, month, and year. As much as in a full-time position, you may find yourself missing out on the growth of your children and grandchildren.

- *Year-round, full-time positions*: President, vice president, judges, sheriffs, district attorneys, governors, state auditors, state controllers, secretaries of state, attorneys general, state superintendents of education, state treasurers, and some legislators: all these are full-time positions entailing heavy, year-round time commitments. A few of these positions pay salaries that come close to matching the private sector, but most pay below or far below market value. Meetings alone often run nine to sixteen hours a day. Add to those the myriad meal-time appointments, homework, and special events. You and your family must be prepared for severe and chronic pressures on your discretionary personal time.

■ **Note** Serving in elected office is not for the weak of heart. Every day requires a passionate commitment to tasks and caring for people who in turn require you to have a great amount of energy to get yourself through the day.

You've got passion and skills. You've identified where your passion and skills match the position for which you'd like to run. Now, make sure that you and your family are willing to invest the time it will take to run the race and do the job.

Identify the Election Cycle and Length of Service

Identify the election cycle for your chosen office. Is the election being held this calendar year? Or is it one, two three, four, or five years away? Study the relevant websites. Go to the relevant election office and ask for a tutorial on the filing procedures and deadlines in the race of interest.

The next question is: how much time are you willing and able to commit to the campaign? A strong local campaign can be waged in one year or less. A strong state-level campaign takes one to two years, and a strong federal level campaign can take two to six years to complete. Some campaigns take many attempts at running for the selected office, which may mean that the length of campaigning can stretch from one to seven years or more.

How much time are you willing to commit to serving in elected office?

Terms are typically two, four, or six years. What is your timeline—and your family's—for serving in elected office? Is it now, and for how long? Your length of term decision will affect your income, your benefits, and your family's well-being. If now is not the time to run, how long will you wait to run and what will you do to get yourself ready to run? Is the right time for you to run five years from now? Although you may not really know at this point, ask yourself: how many terms will I be likely to campaign to serve in office? Some candidates campaign on a platform or promise of "I'll only run twice for this office because I believe in term limits." Some states and positions have term limits, others do not. So, setting a goal for your years in office will help you to focus your campaign message.

Offices for which elections are held every two years include:

- state house
- state senate
- U.S. house
- Some councils and commissions

Offices for which elections are held every four years include:

- president
- vice president
- governor
- mayor
- Some councils and commissions
- sheriff
- judges
- school board
- special district boards

Note Presidential election cycles generally bring out more voters than non-presidential election cycles. Whether your targeted position falls in a presidential election cycle will affect your campaign strategy.

Offices for which elections are held every six years include:

- U.S. senate
- Some judgeships
- Some boards

Pick the Position

At the beginning of this chapter, were you certain that you knew what position you'd be running for? How about now? Is it the same or have you changed your mind?

Once you can confidently state the title of the position for which you are running, you are ready for the following test. Look into a mirror and say: "I am X, and I am running for Y because Z." Now look your spouse or best friend in the eye and say the same thing. Now look at each of your children, no matter their ages, in the eye and say: "I am X, and I am running for Y." You, your family members, and your friends are the ones who will be most immediately and profoundly affected by your decision to run for office. They deserve and desire to hear from you that you are running for office and why.

After you have shared your decision to run for office with your family and friends, it is time to prepare for the rest of the world and the people who will want to know what you are running for and why. So, take some time to practice responding to the questions and remarks in the following scenarios.

"What office are you running for?"

- Smile and give a short reply: "I am X and I'm running for Y." If people want more information, they will ask for it.

- Stand up and shake the person's hand, saying: "I am X and I'm running for Y." At this point, if someone shakes your hand and asks another question, be prepared to give short answers and listen. What people really want is to tell you what they think about the position you are running for and what they want the person in that position to be doing.

- Shake hands with the person and then sit down or kneel down next to the seated person (if the person is in a wheel chair, stay standing until the person invites you to sit down and talk with them) and say: "I am X and I'm running for Y. I'm happy to meet you." Remember to keep your answers short and to spend more time listening than you do talking.

"Oh, I can't vote for you!"

Sometimes you'll hear this remark before the person even knows who you are and why you are running. You know who you are, what you are running for, and where someone must live (and how they must register to vote; see Chapter 5) in order to vote for you. So, your kind and patient reply can be: "I am X and I'm running for Y. Do you live here in Z?" When I ran for Idaho governor, I heard this phrase "I can't vote for you" at state fairs, fundraisers, along parade routes, and at business luncheons for the employees of Idaho companies. Sometimes the response was true—the person lived in another state and truly could not vote for me. Other times the response was a way to walk away from civic duty and my smiling reply was, "Well, remember to vote anyway." Still other times, the response was a thoughtless way of tuning out the discussion. At one business luncheon, I asked a person who had just told me that she couldn't vote for me: "Where do you live?" She replied, "Not here. I live in the next county over." I gave her one of my campaign fliers and said, "I am Jana Kemp, and I'm running for governor of the whole state of Idaho." She accepted the flyer. Keeping people engaged long enough to hear your name and what office you are running for is your goal in every conversation from the start of your campaign until election day.

Conclusion

Matching your passion and time commitment to the position for which you choose to run is critical. Without a proper match, your chances for winning the race diminish. With the right match, voters will hear your genuine passion and will be more likely to believe that you will do what you say you intend to do. When you have chosen the right position that will connect you with voters, they can become your biggest supporters.

With the title of the position you plan to run for in hand, you have one last decision to make before you file to run for office: what political party will you affiliate with when you run? The next chapter will help you examine your assumptions and weigh your alternatives.

Decide to Party or Be Non-Partisan

The two major parties in the United States are the Democratic Party and the Republican Party. As much as we may want and need variety and strength in a third or even more parties, we've got two political party machines that continue to dominate elections at all levels. Successes and frustrations have arisen around party politics throughout the history of our country. The ability of the two parties to work together has also varied over time. Regardless of the parties' ability to work together, what's interesting is that in 2004 the tables of contents for the Republican and Democratic parties' platform documents included the same platform plank titles (as the chapter headings), but each party proposed different actions for achieving their goals. For example, both parties indicated that education was important to them, yet, in the 2011 state legislative and Congressional sessions, we saw just how differently Democrats and Republicans treated unions, teachers, budgets, and citizen protestors.

For some voters, your party affiliation is all they need to know to decide whether or not to vote for you. For other voters, knowing your party is not enough. They want to hear directly from you who you are, what you plan to do, and how you plan to do it. Such voters want to know not only what a candidate's ideas for change are, but also by what specific actions she proposes to implement her ideas.

Your decision whether to affiliate with a party or to be non-partisan is critical to your success. When you decide that there is a party you will affiliate with, you've begun to narrow your elected position options because not every position requires or even allows a party affiliation.

When you pinpoint the elected position for which you want to run, you will also determine whether you will be a non-partisan candidate or declare your party. The choice is yours. Voters have a complex decision to make. They will decide whether to vote for you based on a welter of disparate factors: your party affiliation; whether they think you can win; whether they feel you can do the job, are likeable, and are the person (rather than the party) for whom they want to vote.

Party dominance in an area or state can make it much easier to get elected. Consider this story of a woman who ran a statewide campaign for controller. A highly educated, financially and managerially experienced woman ran her statewide campaign for controller as a member of the state's minority party. Her challenger for the seat had been appointed by the majority-party governor and was herself a member of the majority party. The appointed incumbent was likeable, slightly better known, but less qualified. Yet she won the seat. Being the member of the majority party in an election can help you win, although it is never a guarantee of election success.

Party members may try to recruit you—especially if they think you can win. Yes, both parties scout and recruit winners. Here are two stories as proof. After I filed to run as a Republican for the Idaho House in 2004, a seated Democrat met with me to ask me to run as a Democrat if I didn't win the Republican primary that year (as permitted under Idaho law). I listened, did some research, checked my core values, and replied: "Thanks for asking. No, I won't do that." I went on to win the Republican primary and to win the House seat in the general election that year. Now, flash forward to 2008, when a California Republican woman was fundraising to run for a House seat. Because of the egregious behavior of Republican party members and a variety of other reasons, she opted not to run after all. Democrats saw that she could win the seat and recruited her to run for office as a Democrat, and it worked. She ran as a Democrat and won the House seat she had originally begun campaigning for as a Republican, because the Democratic Party got behind a winnable candidate and worked for the win. Everyone wants a winner.

Political parties are mercurial, fickle, and expedient, so be on guard. One of your challenges in the heat of campaigning will be to stay true to yourself, your values, and your beliefs about how you want to contribute to the future well-being of your community, state, and country. You will need to be aware of what is happening in and around the parties because whether you run as a party candidate or not, you will be affected by all that is happening in a race. Either or any party may choose to play to your ego in order to gain an advantage in a race. A party may choose to recruit you. The party you've chosen to run with may ignore you. If you appear to be a winning candidate, another party may want you even if your beliefs and values don't match that party's platform. Only you can protect yourself, your integrity, and your reputation. Stay vigilant about what the political parties are really maneuvering to achieve with you—or without you.

Partisan and Non-Partisan Positions

You've made your partisan or non-partisan decision. Now, revisit which position is the best match for you. The following two groups of positions are typically non-partisan and partisan, respectively. Be sure to check with your local elections clerk or your state election office to confirm the details for the position that is of most interest to you.

Non-partisan positions are typically (but not invariably) found in and on the following: school organizations; school boards; trade and civic organizations; water, soil, and conservation boards; utility boards; councils; and commissions. Mayors and judges may also be non-partisan.

Partisan positions typically (but not invariably) include the following:

- Precinctman—Democrats and Republicans have elected precinct workers. Sometimes the elections are on primary ballots, sometimes the elections are held only within party meetings and caucus events.
- County assessor
- County clerk
- County or parish commissioner
- State treasurer/controller
- Secretary of state
- Attorney general
- Lieutenant governor

- Governor
- State representative
- State senator
- U.S. representative
- U.S. senator
- Vice president
- President

Your Party Affiliation Decision

Make your decision as to your party affiliation in full light of your convictions, research, reflection, judgment, and resolve. As part of this deliberative process, ask yourself the following questions:

- Am I running to win, regardless of my personal values and beliefs? Am I prepared to modify my positions on issues and even flip-flop as political expediency dictates? If winning is your singular objective, the advantages of running for the majority party in your election district will likely predominate.

- Am I running based on my values and beliefs and planning to stay true to them throughout the election cycle? If so, research which party most closely matches who you are.

- Am I committed to holding a partisan position for which I will have to declare a party? If so, pick the party that most closely matches who you are and what you represent.

- Will I proudly announce the party with which I am affiliated? If not, consider running for a non-partisan position.

- Am I committed to remaining non-partisan? If so, identify which elective positions are available to non-partisan candidates in your election district.

- Am I committed to a partisan position yet desirous of remaining free of party affiliations? If so, consult your election office to determine what your options are and what procedure you must follow to get on the ballot. More on this option in Chapter 5.

One of the questions in the quiz you took in Chapter 2 concerned how you felt about announcing your political party to the world. This is the time to revisit that question and reflect again on your answers. Running for office requires perfect clarity on the question of your party affiliation.

Question: *What's your take on declaring a party?*

Possible answers:

- *I prefer to keep my political party affiliation to myself.*
  YES: In most states, elective judges, sheriffs, council/commission/board members, and mayors, either must be or may be non-partisan positions. Exceptionally, Nebraska's unicameral state legislature is mandatorily non-partisan.

- *I am happy to announce my political party affiliation and to run as a party candidate.*
  YES: State and federal legislative and executive elected offices and some mayors and commission seats are predominantly filled by partisan candidates.

- *I am convinced the political party system is not working and will declare to run as an independent candidate.*
  YES: Most states allow independent candidates in every race. However, the rules for an independent to get on the ballot are different in every state and in some states "independent" is a political party. More about getting onto the ballot in Chapter 5.

Now consider another round of hypothetical statements about your political credo to help you refine which party you want to affiliate with, or whether you will choose any party at all:

1. *I believe that government must play a significant role in providing for the infrastructure and human needs of this country. Taxes are appropriate funding sources.*

   - Yes: Democrat, Socialist, or Communist.

   - No: Go to next question.

2. *I believe that government is too involved in too many things and needs to get out and stay out of our way as business owners and as human beings. We'd all be better off without taxes.*

   - Yes: Republican, Constitutionalist, or Libertarian.

   - No: Go to next question.

3. *I believe that the current two-party system of control in this country is not working and that single-issue candidates cannot solve the problems of this country nor prepare us for a bright future.*

   - *Yes*: Independent or Moderate.

   - *No*: Go to next question.

4. *I believe that political parties and positions are not a fit for me and would prefer to be a non-partisan candidate in a non-partisan position.*

   - *Yes*: Most judgeships and many council, mayoral, and commission seats are non-partisan.

   - *No*: Go to next question.

5. *I believe that single issues must be addressed first in order for the well-being of the country to improve.*

   - *Yes*: Identify the issue that causes you to want to run for office. Research which party or parties are a match for you and your message. Keep researching to make your party affiliation decision.

   - *No*: If you have answered "no" to all five of these questions, keep doing research in this chapter and in the variety of places that will help you make your decision. Then come back and take this quiz again. Without clarity on the question of party, your candidacy is officially over. As you'll learn in Chapter 5, every office requires a declaration of partisan or non-partisan affiliation.

Note Each party has its strengths that can lead the country forward to success. Every party has its weaknesses that may stand in the way of this country's future success. You must decide how you will, or will not, affiliate with a political party.

Political Parties in the United States of America

Political parties are those entities registered with each state's elections office and with the Federal Election Commission for the purpose of running candidates for elected office. In alphabetical order, the following political parties fielded presidential candidates in the 2008 election cycle:

- Boston Tea Party/Personal Choice Party
- Constitution Party
- Democratic Party
- Green Party
- Independent/New American Independent Party
- Independent/Independent Ecology Party/Natural Law Party
- Libertarian Party
- Party for Socialism and Liberation
- Prohibition Party
- Reform Party
- Republican Party
- Socialist Party USA
- Socialist Workers Party

In addition to these nationally active parties, other parties are active at state and lower levels of elected government. In any given election cycle, some fifty political parties, many of an evanescent, unstable, or provocative character, are registered and active in the United States. Learn more about what the parties are, what they stand for, and where you fit into the beliefs and values of each. If you opt to affiliate with a third party or to have no party affiliation, know that your road to a win will be even more challenging, as I learned in my independent run for Idaho Governor in 2010. Consult your state and county election offices as to which parties are recognized in your county and state. If a party is not recognized, it may prevent you from being on the ballot.

Invest enough time in research that you can confidently determine whether a dominant party, nationally active party, or an issue-focused state party affiliation is the best match for you. Moreover, explore the political philosophy spectrum to test the degrees of congruence between your own political philosophy and the political philosophies espoused by the various parties. By convention, most of the bandwidth on the American political spectrum is assigned to the liberal left, the moderate middle, and the conservative right. Here's a crash course.

The Political Left or Liberal Philosophies

Recall from the quiz in this chapter that holding the belief that government must play a significant role in providing for the infrastructure and human needs of this country and that taxes are appropriate funding sources is a political left or liberal set of philosophies. Caring for the environment at the expense of business opportunities, wanting to spend more money on public schools and to pay teachers more every year, as well as insisting on national healthcare, round out this philosophical end of the continuum. The most active left or liberal parties include the Communist, Socialist, and Democratic parties.

The Political Moderate Philosophies

Some people argue that to claim to be moderate is to have no opinion or to be a fence-sitter. This is not true for people who have done their research and have decided that on some issues they lean left while on others they lean right. For example, a moderate Republican is one who describes him- or herself as someone focused on fiscal responsibility and social concerns such as the environment and education. A blue-dog Democrat is traditionally fiscally conservative and social-issue focused. In reality, the moderate philosophies are pragmatic on almost all issues. In other words, a moderate position is more likely to be able to solve problems than to get stuck in left or right political rhetoric that prevents finding solutions for the problems and challenges we face.

The "middle" can be confusing to candidates and voters alike. This is why it is critical for you to know why you are running and whether you are running with, or without, a party affiliation. People will ask you, "What does that mean?" on a regular basis. Your answer must be so clear that you can convince people that you know what you are talking about, even if listeners choose not to vote for you. The politically moderate parties include the moderate and, sometimes, the independent.

The Political Right or Conservative Philosophies

People and parties holding political right or conservative philosophies believe that government is too involved in too many things and needs to get out and stay out of our way as business owners and as human beings. This philosophy set also believes we would all be better off without taxes and that in fact taxes may be unconstitutional. The far right cares more for business opportunities than protecting the environment, wants to spend less money on public schools (and even hopes that public schools might be done away with), and proclaims national healthcare unconstitutional. The most active parties representing the right or conservative philosophies are the Republican, Libertarian (allowing that some radical libertarian laissez-faire beliefs coincide with liberal beliefs), and Constitutional parties.

The Political Independents—Not Necessarily Parties

Choosing to run as an independent can be confusing, with a great deal depending on the whether the word *independent* is capitalized. As a 2008 presidential candidate, Ralph Nader ran in most states as an unaffiliated independent, but in some states for ad hoc electoral reasons he also ran as the candidate of the Independent Party. When I ran for Idaho governor in 2010, I ran as an independent, completely free of any party affiliation; yet my candidacy was endorsed by vote of the membership of the New American Independent Party, which in 2011 changed its name to the Citizens Party of the United States. Determine what your election offices at local and state levels rule on the independent front.

Issue-Driven Parties

Issue-driven parties continually pop up and fade away all along the political philosophy continuum. People who are more passionate about causes and issues, and about making statements rather than winning elections, tend to run with an issue-driven party. From the United States Pirate Party, United States Marijuana Party, and Populist Party on the left through the Jefferson Republican Party and the Objectivist Party on the right, you'll find a party for nearly every issue and ideology. Once again, the key is to spend enough time researching where your beliefs and values fit so that you are very clear about the party you choose.

Exponents of parties on opposite ends of the political philosophy spectrum sometimes vote the same way on particular issues, albeit for different reasons. While serving as an Idaho state representative, I saw the House's most conservative and most liberal female representatives—the one a gun-toter and the other an openly gay school teacher—vote the same way on a bill I had assumed they'd split on. Stay on your toes and on your game during the research, campaign, and office-holding phases of your life.

Not Always a Political Party

Distinct from registered political parties, there are many groups in the U.S. that nonetheless engage in political commentary and activity that is explicitly or implicitly aligned for or against particular candidates. Business groups, corporations, church groups, chambers of commerce, unions, political action committees, and professional groups may endorse and directly or indirectly support or oppose candidates running with registered political parties. Be aware of the legal and political differences between a political party and a politically active group. If you affiliate with a political group that is not a political party and you want to run as a candidate for office, you may find yourself surprised when the election office says you are not eligible to run under that group name. Do the research. Find out whether your locality or state recognizes a group in which you are interested as a political party.

Party Affiliation? Pros and Cons

If you plan to run for a non-partisan position, you do not have to choose a political party. However, you may choose to affiliate with a party in order to get financial and campaign infrastructure support that is often difficult to secure on your own. Be sure to check with your election offices to learn what rules and laws govern non-partisan races.

If you plan to run for a partisan position, you still have a choice about whether to declare a party affiliation or whether to run without a party affiliation. Here are some of the pros and cons. These potential pluses and minuses may not affect which party you choose. However, they may affect how you allow yourself to be involved in the party you choose.

The Pros

Party affiliation pros begin with the statistical fact that Democratic and Republican party-affiliated candidates are most often the winners of partisan races. So the first advantage of running with a major party affiliation is that you'll have a better chance of winning your partisan race.

Another pro is that voters feel they can more easily understand who you are and what you are about when you affiliate with a party. Running for office as a party member helps define who you are in voters' minds. The working assumption is that if you are running with a party, you believe what the members of that party believe. Be aware, however, that this is not always true.

There are candidates who choose to run with a party purely because they believe that their chances of winning are much greater, rather than truly assimilating to the beliefs and values of the party they have declared as "theirs."

Caucuses and/or primaries are a part of the election process when you run as a partisan candidate. This election process is a positive because it helps voters and contributors learn more about you. You have an opportunity to hone your message and to be tested by a rigorous interrogation process. You also gain more media coverage when there are more races before the general election.

Media coverage is much greater when you run with the Democratic or Republican parties. It is really this simple. Some media sources may cover third-party and independent candidates in some races. However, most media outlets remain focused on making news for the majority parties.

Campaign organization and workers are available when you run with a party. However, just because you've affiliated with the party doesn't mean you'll get any support during a primary race. Sometimes, even after you've won a primary, you are not guaranteed help from the party. Within every party, there are also politics of personality and questions of "are you Republican enough" or "are you Democratic enough" influencing whether you'll get party support. The perfect scenario of course is that you win the primary and/or are the chosen candidate during a caucus, and the party does get behind you to help in all ways, including fundraising.

Campaign fundraising is usually much easier when you run as a party candidate. In some states, party-affiliated candidates can, by law, raise more money for their races than can independent, non-party-affiliated candidates. The playing field is definitely skewed in favor of the majority party member Democrats and Republicans.

The Cons

Parties have pecking orders. This means that if you haven't already been involved as a party worker, a precinct person, or previously run for office with the party, you may get the cold shoulder, while someone who has already paid the party dues gets all of the attention—even if their officeholding skills don't measure up to yours.

Parties place expectations on you that you may not like. If you get elected, you may be expected to fundraise for the party, to contribute to the party and to other candidates, and to endorse other candidates from the same party.

There will always be things with which you disagree. No matter what party or non-party-affiliation choice you make, there will be individual actions and/or party platform planks with which you will disagree. Your challenge is in figuring out what you can and cannot live with during the time you campaign for and hold office.

Consider my decisions to run as a Republican twice, and then to run as an independent for a higher office. My decision to run as an independent for governor was based on the fact that I had amassed a long list of reasons the Idaho Republican party had left me. The final straw that tipped my decision to sever my affiliation was the lawsuit that the Idaho Republican Party filed against the state of Idaho to close the primaries. Being philosophically opposed to taking people's right to vote away when taxpayers are footing the electoral bill prompted me to review my beliefs and voting record.

During my critical reflection and self-assessment, I discovered that I had always voted for the person and not the party; had always done my homework and voted on bills based on their merit and their focus on highest good for the whole of the state; and had a proven voting record of saying no, even when party members and the governor's office were twisting my arm to vote with them and cast a yes vote. My decision was to stay true to my beliefs, values, and record. My obvious choice was to run as an independent candidate, which in Idaho is non-partisan and not a party affiliation. Was running as an independent harder than running as a party member? Yes. It meant much less media coverage, fundraising challenges, and no established campaign organization. But from the standpoint of being clear about why I was running, what I had to offer the state, and divorcing myself and my reputation from the poor behaviors I repeatedly saw in action within the Idaho Republican party, it was easy to run as a non-partisan independent.

Non-Partisan: Some Definitions

To be non-partisan means that you do not declare a party, do not talk about being affiliated with a party, and do not share what party you would be affiliated with if you had chosen a party. Yet, in many non-partisan races across the country, candidates do choose to disclose their party leanings. The move toward party politicization of non-partisan positions makes it difficult for candidates and voters alike to remain focused on the good decision making that is required for the good of a community.

In judicial elections, non-partisanship is the norm, though not universal. In some states and for some offices, openly campaigning and stating your positions on issues can get you disqualified from the race. Non-partisan offices may require candidates to observe strict neutrality and non-disclosure with respect to party affiliation and personal beliefs. Once again, meet with your election office officials to learn what non-partisan means legally and in campaign practices.

■ **Note** Without clarity on the question of party, your candidacy is officially over.

Conclusion

Whether you choose to affiliate with a political party or to remain non-partisan, you can always change your mind later. Notice how neither the Democratic nor the Republican establishments dwell on the fact that Ronald Reagan and Rick Perry were Democrats before they became Republican governors. Witness too Senator Lieberman's transformation from unsuccessful Democratic vice presidential candidate to successful "Connecticut for Lieberman" independent senatorial candidate. People at all levels have found themselves disenchanted or inconvenienced by one party, and have switched to another. So, make your choice, know why you've made it, be able to defend it, and run your race.

File to Run

You've decided for what office you'd most like to put your hat in the ring. It's time to file. That's right. You must file paperwork to declare that you are in the race. Filing to run is a step that is both a legal statement and a personal statement about your intentions to run for office. Filing to run allows you to go public with the announcement of your candidacy and to begin collecting money for your campaign. Failure to properly file prevents you from being a serious candidate and may even prevent you from entering the race at all.

Filing for office is like passing "go," because it enables you to launch your campaign. Check with your elections office(s) to determine how many steps are required for you to file. Some election districts and states have a one-step filing, and others have multiple-step filing.

▨ **Note** Be a serious and competent candidate. Properly file to run for office so that the media and voters will be more likely to take your candidacy seriously.

Choose Your Treasurer and File Your Paperwork

You've gotten this far. You've decided what office you will run for. You've clarified why you are running. You've determined what, if any, party affiliation you will declare. You are ready to begin campaigning, but, before you begin, you must file the proper paperwork with the election office(s) that oversee the race in which you wish to participate. In addition to having your personal information in hand for the filing, you'll need to have the name, address, email and telephone number of your treasurer along with your treasurer's signature so that the election office can verify that the person has in fact agreed to be your campaign treasurer.

- *Treasurer selection.* After the candidate, the campaign treasurer is the biggest job in any campaign. The treasurer is co-responsible with the candidate for complying with all legal requirements for tracking campaign money and filing reports. You'll want a treasurer who is capable with numbers and able to manage details. You'll want someone who is organized. You'll want a person you trust. Your treasurer most often ends up knowing more about your campaign finances than any other person on your team. Your treasurer's name is on the line, right along with yours. Choose a treasurer who can take the pressure of your candidacy and manage the details of the campaign finances and reporting.

- *One-step filing.* In the one-step filing process, you file the paperwork that declares who you are, for what office you are running, and who your treasurer is. The one-step filing process is most commonly found in elections for special election districts, school boards, and city and county offices. After you file in a one-step process, you participate in the general election for that seat.

- *Multiple-step filing.* A multiple-step filing process includes some or all of the following steps:

  1. File your paperwork with the appropriate election office, to establish that you are a candidate or are considering candidacy, and to identify your treasurer. Remember, this is a legal step with legal implications. It dictates with whom you may discuss campaign matters, how you begin raising money, and about whether you are a legal candidate in the race in which you wish to participate.
  2. Declare the office title for which you are running and your party affiliation, if any. This step is sometimes merged with the first step; other times it constitutes a separate filing. For example, in 2009, I filed my candidacy intentions as an independent candidate and listed my treasurer's name without naming the office for which I would be running. A month later, when my campaign team was in place, I returned to the elections office in the Idaho Secretary of State's Office to file the name of the office—governor—for which I would run.

3. In some elections, you must collect signatures to ensure your name is on the ballot. Check with your election office to see whether you are required to collect and file verified signature petitions to get your name on the ballot.

4. Along with your campaign activities and balloting experiences, you must file campaign reports. Campaign reports are essentially financial reports showing what you've collected from whom and what you've spent with whom. For some local-level offices, the paperwork is fairly manageable. The bigger the election district and the higher the seat you are pursuing, the more rigorous the paperwork and filing calendar become. The report-filing requirements are another reason you want to have a good working relationship with the elections office(s) for your race. Federal reporting is the most rigorous. Federal reports are scanned, scoured, and analyzed by so many people that one error can potentially cost a candidate an election.

5. In many states, you must participate in a caucus process. A party holds a caucus for the purpose of thinning the candidate field down to one party-endorsed candidate. Depending on the state, caucuses are used in all races, only in select races, or not used at all. Often the caucus-winning party-endorsed candidate goes on to win a primary election, but not always. The caucus tool is designed to lead to the party-identified and -endorsed candidate being on the primary election ballot.

6. Participate in a primary election (except in elections that bypass primaries and go directly to a general election). This is the race that will put you onto the general election ballot. Primaries may occur from two months to ten months before a general election ballot. After winning a primary race, most election offices send you a certificate of election indicating that you are now qualified to be on the general election ballot. The distance between your primary and general election races will affect your campaign plans, strategies, and actions (more on this in Chapter 6).

7. Complete the general election race. This is the race that will put you into office. Whether you win or lose the general election, you'll still have reports to file. In fact, you'll continue to have reports to file until you close your campaign and campaign accounts. More on this in Chapters 13 and 14.

Locate Election Offices

Each of the seven steps in the preceding section is overseen by the pertinent election office(s). As we have stressed repeatedly, it is imperative that you locate and consult the pertinent election offices and officers as soon as you become serious about running for office. Most election offices—whether special district, board, municipal, county, or state—have dedicated websites. The website of the Federal Election Commission—www.fec.gov—is an essential portal for all campaigns for federal office.

Get to know the election office team on a first-name basis. Each person in an election office has valuable information and can coach you on the filing steps and requirements for getting your name onto a ballot. Some election offices hold workshops for candidates and treasurers for the purpose of explaining the filing rules, the required paperwork, the filing calendars, and special reporting requirements.

■ **Note** Get to know your election office team members. They have a wealth of knowledge that can help you successfully navigate the paperwork that comes with being a candidate.

Understand the Legalities

Many sections of state and federal law apply to the process of running for elected office. If you fail to meet the legal requirements of running for office, you are out of the race. If you fail to comply with the laws and reporting rules, you are out of the race. Here are some of the legalities that can put you out of the race. When you are compliant, you can keep yourself in the race.

- *Residency Requirements*: Many offices have residency requirements. You may have to live in a certain neighborhood or district to enter the race. You may have to have lived in that certain area for one or more years to qualify to run. (Recall that Hillary Clinton announced her New York residency before her husband had left the Oval Office, which allowed her to run for U.S. Senator from New York.) Check with your elections office to be certain that you have met any and all residency requirements. You don't want this to be the impediment that prevents you from running for office, so be sure that you are in full compliance.

- *Filings*: This chapter provides a level of information that will start you on the right path. It is not itself a legal document. Be sure to meet with your elections office(s) to get all of the information you will need to file and report accurately and punctually for your race.

- *Handling Monies*: We'll delve into this in more detail in Chapter 8, but for now here are the big things to know:

  - There are limits on how much money you can accept and from whom.

  - There are set-date reports that must be filed.

  - There are dollar-amount triggers that require special reports.

  - Political contributions are not tax-deductible.

  - You must keep very detailed records and keep copies of everything you turn in to your election office.

- *Giveaways*: What you can give away during your campaign varies by federal race and state race laws. In some states you can give away a pencil, bumper sticker, or yard sign with your name on it. In other states you may NOT give away those items during your campaign without a purchase having been made and proper paperwork filed. This is another category that requires you to research what is allowed in your race.

- *Information Disclosures*: Disclosures are most rigorous for federal offices. At the federal level, you are asked to disclose your personal and family net worth, to share where you and your spouse are employed and how much money you make, and hundreds of other questions. In local races, the information disclosure requirement may be as simple as your address and your contact information. In regional and state level races, the information disclosure requirements vary. Keep researching what the requirements for your race include.

- *Ethics*: Laws govern much of your campaign decisionmaking. For most of us, a sense of personal ethics also enters the campaign. Will your campaign participate in the mudslinging that so many political consultants advise wins races? Or will you stay above the fray, insisting on no mudslinging and sticking to relevant facts? Another ethical consideration: will you and your campaign serve alcohol? Yes, this has legal implications, too. If your campaign served the alcohol that allowed someone to leave your event too drunk to drive, and the person got into an accident and was cited for drunk driving, then your campaign is very likely legally liable. Consider what your own ethics are and how you'll rely on your ethics to guide your campaign.

- When in doubt, ask questions of your elections office, or of an attorney. You'll want to be as informed as possible about the legal ramifications of running for office and managing your campaign.

Note Just because it is legal doesn't mean it is ethical. Identify for yourself and your team what will be acceptable behavior and decision making for your campaign. Communicate clearly to your team what you will expect and accept.

Know the Sunshine Laws

The laws governing campaigns are typically called "sunshine laws," because, in 1976, the government passed the Sunshine Act, which was designed to support freedom of information and to create greater transparency in government. In addition to this federal act, states have also passed sunshine laws to keep government and the election process open and transparent. Ask your elections office(s) for a copy of the sunshine laws that govern your race. In some cases you will find them online. In others, you will need to go in person to the election office to track down a copy of the laws you must follow to run your campaign. Stay current because election laws and rules change from year to year as they are amended by legislatures and regulatory authorities. Sunshine laws and election rules include the following:

1. *Who is required to report*: You and your campaign treasurer will have to file reports. So will political action committees, political parties, people and organizations making independent expenditures on behalf of candidates, people distributing electioneering communications, and others.

2. *Residency requirements*: These vary depending on the race.

3. *How much money you can accept*: Contribution limits vary depending on the state, the race, the level of the race, and even on the party or with which you may affiliate.

4. *From whom you can accept money or in-kind contributions*: Be sure everyone on your team is informed about this key variable.

5. *What you can give away*: The items you can give away for free vary by state. Find out what rules govern your giveaways.

6. *When you can campaign*: This is largely tied to when you have filed and filed completely as well as the timeline of caucus, primary, and general elections in your state.

7. *When you must file reports*: Each election office manages an election cycle calendar that includes when reports must be filed, when you must file to run for office, when you must file to continue a campaign, and when you must file to close a campaign.

8. *Voting and absentee voting*: Learn what the laws specify regarding voting and absentee voting in your election. Some states require voter identification for casting a ballot. Other election jurisdictions do not. Some elections allow for absentee voting by mail, others allow for mail-in ballots as well as voting in person at a specific location. Absentee votes are a growing percentage of any given total vote count, so learn when and how absentee voters can get ballots.

Choose Your Campaign Team

Start choosing the members of your campaign team. After identifying the campaign treasurer, find your campaign manager. The campaign manager is responsible for helping you win. In some races and depending on applicable filing rules and sunshine laws, you can be the candidate, the treasurer, and the campaign manager. For some candidates—especially for local positions in small-district races—this works, and they win their races. However, for many candidates, juggling two or more "jobs" in a race is simply too much and prevents a win. My advice is that, no matter how small your election district, you should focus on being the candidate, and you should identify a treasurer and a campaign manager to support you.

Your campaign manager will oversee and coordinate your campaign's messaging, advertising, recruitment of endorsements, event schedule, fundraising schedule, calendar, safety planning, and budget. A campaign manager can be a volunteer or a paid staff member. If you pay staff, be sure to follow all employment laws. Finding the right campaign manager will require several conversations with several people. Just as you looked for specific skills in your treasurer, you'll want your campaign manager to have specific skills, including the following:

- *Organization and project-management skills*: Campaigns are complex projects with fixed deadlines, so organization skills are a must. One missed deadline can break the campaign.

- *Management skills*: Every campaign relies on volunteers. Some campaigns have paid staff. A campaign manager must have great people skills so that you keep your team together and working for your win.

- *Knowledge of the politics in your race*: Having a campaign manager who knows the nuances of the race and the people in it will help you strategize what needs to be in your campaign plan and what needs to happen day after day during the campaign.

- *Knowledge of where you need to go to meet the volume of people who need to know your name and that you are in the race*: Getting in front of people face-to-face and shaking hands is a critical part of your daily calendar. Your campaign manager can help line up where you need to be day after day. For instance, in one election cycle my campaign manager took me to the horse track because she knew that there were eligible voters there whom I wasn't meeting at my usual venues.

- *Ability to delegate and to ensure work gets done*: Delegation skills ensure that volunteers stay engaged in helping the campaign. Delegation skills also require follow-up to ensure people will be where they've committed to being and will get the work done and delivered on time. A candidate is only as good as her campaign team, which is only as good as its campaign manager. For instance, a team member who embezzles money from your campaign tarnishes you and your campaign. On the other hand, a team member recognized as a positive community contributor can enhance your campaign.

Be Prepared Before Announcing Your Candidacy

The best strategy for announcing your candidacy is to be prepared. Being prepared includes having chosen your treasurer and having filed your paperwork with the proper elections office. Remember the legal ramifications of not having your paperwork in order before announcing your candidacy. Keep yourself in the race by being prepared on all legal fronts when filing to run for office.

Your preparation also requires that the following logistics be worked out and available for public release. Contributors, the media, and voters will want access to all of these contact particulars of your campaign:

- *Campaign Phone Number*: Will you use your home phone? Will you use your cell phone? Will you establish a new, campaign-only phone number? When making this decision, consider how many people may end up calling you. The bigger your election district and number of voters in your race, the more you'll want to have a campaign-only telephone number and reserve the use of your cell-phone for campaign team members only.

- *Campaign Mailing Address*: Candidacy paperwork typically requests a residence address and a mailing address along with a mailing address for your treasurer. What address will you list publically for the receipt of campaign mail?

- *Campaign Office*: Will you have one? Where? Will it be your house? Will it be open to the public, or is it only for campaign team members? How will you ensure the safety of that office?

- *Campaign Email Address*: What email address will be listed on literature, on webpages, and on correspondence? Will you respond to emails? If not, who will respond to emails and letters?

- *Campaign Website*: Establishing a website and other social media pages before you announce your candidacy is helpful for gaining immediate traction for name recognition and fundraising. I did not announce my candidacy for governor until I had a functioning web page that was capable of accepting contributions.

Other essential elements of your campaign preparation include:

- *Campaign treasurer's public role defined*: Is he or she expected to attend fundraising events? Or will all treasurer's work be done without taking an in-person public role in the campaign?

- *Campaign manager's public role defined*: Can your manager answer questions on your behalf? If so, which ones? Will your campaign manager attend most events with you to help manage your time and to get you from one event to another?

- *Family member roles defined*: Is it to smile, shake hands, and wave? Will it include answering questions on your behalf, or not?

- *Smile and shake hands*: This is your job. It is also the job of everyone on your campaign team. Be prepared to smile even when you don't want to, even when you are exhausted, and even when faced with an angry constituent.

Your level of preparation will set the tone for your entire campaign, for your campaign team, for the volunteers you hope to recruit, and for the voters whose votes you are working to earn. Any shortcuts or short-comings in planning can grow into headaches and even nightmares once the campaign is underway.

Conclusion

Be sure to follow the rules for filing and reporting. If you can't follow these rules, people are less likely to trust your ability to do the job you are campaigning to do. Many candidates have been knocked out of races for failure to comply with the rules of filing, running, and reporting. Do the ongoing homework required for your campaign to comply with all of the filing and campaigning rules and to hit all of the reporting deadlines. With your paperwork and pre-announcement decisions in order, you can focus your energies on the daily details of getting your name in front of voters, which is what the next seven chapters on running describe.

Run: Create Campaign Plans

You've filed paperwork to run for office. You've officially begun your campaign. Now it is time to outline your campaign plan. What will you do each day? How will you interact with the media? How much money do you need to raise? These are some of the questions you'll tackle while creating your campaign plan.

The value of having a campaign plan cannot be overstated. Your plan may be as straightforward as, "Win the seat by recruiting enough volunteers to help get the word out and to earn votes for me." Or, your plan may have hundreds of moving parts, pieces, and considerations. Whatever the size and complexity of your plan, it guides your decision making, scheduling, and the activities of your campaign team. Your campaign plan will help you stay on budget and on schedule. Your campaign plan will help your team stay on message, on track, and on task.

Every campaign plan has a level of detail that allows you and the team to know what to do when. Every campaign plan also requires a degree of flexibility such that the unexpected opportunities and challenges that arise can be worked into the plan. Simple campaign plans work well for local elections: raise money, gather some volunteers, put up signs, get your candidacy in the news, and get out the vote. Win.

Complex plans are needed for election districts with large populations or territories. The more ground you have to cover, the more complex your campaign plan and calendar will be.

Although a campaign plan will inevitably undergo some revision along the way, resist the impulse to revise it every week. Your team needs to be able to work the plan over time before you redirect their focus and change what you are asking them to get done. One of my team's discoveries, for example, was that we were not raising enough funds for the time we invested in hosting events. So, we dropped fundraising events in favor of online and personal-ask fundraising. The changed approach saved us time and netted better financial results.

Note Your campaign plan is your tool for getting elected. Without a plan, volunteers and staff will not know how or where to jump in and help. With a plan, tasks can be clearly assigned and accomplished.

Formulate the Big Picture

Start your campaign plan with the big picture. What are you trying to accomplish and why? "Obviously," you say, "I want to win." So do all of the other people in the race. Remember, what voters want to know is why you are running and how your winning will be of benefit to them. Your big-picture campaign plan must answer these questions:

- *How many voters do we have to reach to get a winning vote count?* To determine this number, study the past voting history for your race. Election offices have this information to share.

- *Where are the biggest concentrations of likely voters?* This will help you know where to spend your time and resources. What neighborhoods, villages, towns, or cities do they live in? What meetings do they attend that you can also attend?

- *What do your voters care about and want you to address?* What's your message to them? More on honing your message in Chapter 7.

- *How much money will you need to raise?* More on fundraising in Chapter 8.

- *How many volunteers do you need to recruit? What will they be asked to do?* Be sure to define what their delegated tasks are, when they need to be done, and to share any details or rules that will guide completion.

- *How will your family and friends participate in the campaign?* Some will become active members of your volunteer team. Others will confine their support to writing much-appreciated checks. For still others, the answer will be, "I'm cheering, but not getting involved."

Create a Strategic Plan

With your big picture in mind, it is now time to create a strategic plan that includes the details for winning your race and a timeline or calendar that directs you and the entire campaign team on a daily, weekly, and monthly basis. Some candidates include a strengths, weaknesses, opportunities, and threat analysis (SWOT) for themselves and each of the candidates in the race in order to create points of difference for themselves and their messaging. A SWOT analysis can also help you differentiate yourself among the field of candidates.

A campaign plan is your strategic plan for how you'll get voters to vote for you. A campaign platform is a statement of the things you stand for and the reasons you are running for office, as well as the values, beliefs, and issues that you want to address during the race and when in office. A campaign platform gives people reasons to vote for you.

Additionally, some candidates choose to include detailed topic analysis, along with candidate analysis, in their plan. Others opt to not pursue this level of detail. Whatever you choose to document as your campaign plan, be sure that it helps you get out and meet voters. Whether you use software or hard-copy project charts, the complexity of managing a campaign requires that project-management skills and tools be implemented effectively. Our team used a combination of emails, committees, task-lists and calendars, within our campaign plan to guide our efforts. Without strong organization, the campaign plan fails. All the plans in the world don't matter if you never get out and meet voters to ask for their votes.

Target Your Voters

In every election race there are targeted voters. For instance, not everyone who is eligible to vote is even registered to vote. So, ask your election office how many people are registered to vote in the district/parish/region in which you are running. Further, out of the registered voters, there are people who will vote for you, people who may vote for you, and people who will never vote for you. Identifying who falls into which category can be challenging. However, there are resources to tap to identify which voters are most important to reach.

For instance, if you are running as a Democrat, it is unlikely you'll get a core Republican voter to vote for you. Conversely, a core Democratic voter is unlikely to vote for a Republican. As a party candidate, you'll want to work with your party on the lists it can generate for you. Both parties keep detailed voter records and address lists. Both parties can create mailing lists, neighborhood walk lists, and maps. Both parties can assist you in indentifying who is most likely to vote in any given year and who may be most likely to vote for you. If you are running as an independent or unaffiliated candidate, you can still conduct an analysis of voters to see where the votes have fallen in the past, and where you should invest your time.

One way of identifying the voters you want to reach is to research answers to the following questions, using relevant maps, demographic and psephological statistical analyses, address lists in public election office and party records, as well as anecdotal research via interviews with election officers, party officials, and journalists:

- *Where is the greatest concentration of people who tend to vote for the party with whom I'm running?*

- *Where is the greatest discontent with incumbents and how can I reach their constituents?*

- *Where is the greatest concentration of people I might convert to voting for me? What neighborhoods do they live in? What groups do they belong to?*

- *Where are the people that I must convert to voting for me in order to win the election? What groups do they belong to?*

- *Who and where are the absentee voters?*

With answers to these questions, your campaign team can create annotated GIS-layered walking maps of the groups and individuals you need to meet: by street, trade-group, city, and many other criteria.

To help you build your own campaign plan, I offer the following campaign plan of mine as a sample:

SAMPLE CAMPAIGN PLAN

Campaign Outcome/Goal:

Jana Kemp elected as Governor of Idaho, November 2, 2010.

Objectives in support of this goal:

1. Get onto the general ballot by following all of the necessary steps for doing so.

2. Garner 250,000 votes on November 2, 2010 in order to win the election. (This number is based on analysis of past gubernatorial elections and what it will take in 2010 to win the race.)

3. Develop a base of contributors that will generate the needed resources to conduct all necessary campaign activities: $750,000 is the budgeted goal. (This amount is determined by analyzing past race spending and spending by Minnesota Governor Jesse Ventura, who as an independent candidate spent $400,000 in his winning election.

4. Develop a statewide volunteer pool that will implement campaign tasks ranging from event hosting and support to flyer delivery and yard-sign postings and clean-up.

5. Establish a core campaign team.

Key Campaign Message:

"Empower Idaho! We have the brainpower and resources to make Idaho as great a place to work as it is to live so that every generation can look forward to a bright and sustainable future. What we need is leadership in the governor's office. It's time to put the political elite cowboys on the stagecoach out of town."

Primary Campaign Platform:

Education

To provide cost-effective, efficient education programs—pre-K, K-12, college, and university—that meet or exceed federal, state, and local expectations by 2020, we need:

- Well-trained, certified professionals providing early childhood education that successfully prepares our children for entering kindergarten

- Public elementary and secondary education providers who have the staff, resources, and facilities they need to provide the free public education our state constitution guarantees to every Idaho citizen

- Affordable, accessible colleges and universities

- Efficient, frugal, focused public education administration from the smallest rural elementary school to the State Board of Education

- Higher-education research programs whose discoveries are monetizable and transferable to the marketplace

Entrepreneurial Economic Development

Now is the time to discover and support the businesses in garages, shops, and barns around Idaho that can become the next generation of job-providers here. More effective public/private partnerships with our universities to create greater speed and efficiency in making marketable discoveries and developments are a critical part of our state's future success. By 2012, we will know what our statewide business potentials are and we will have begun to see measurable job growth. The goal is to create jobs and businesses that will put stability back into our economy and provide futures for our children. We must:

- Utilize a blend of the best traditional farming practices and agricultural innovations to create new, improved, and sustainable marketable processes, equipment, and products that lead the world's farming and ranching industries.

- Create incentives and reduce the barriers for forming new and expanding Idaho-based businesses.

- Facilitate bringing the right people and the right resources together at the right time to capitalize on Idaho's brainpower and put our great state on the world economic map.

- Become an international leader in energy innovation.

- Meet our own consumption demands using ecologically and economically sustainable methods.

- Successfully expand safe, reliable, and cost-effective energy sources that are available in the marketplace and that maximize efficient use of resources by 2014.

- Additional areas of potential innovations with market viability run the gamut of high-technology, ag-tech, biotech, film and the arts, education, and food processing.

Effective, Efficient State Services

The state of Idaho currently operates 14 executive offices and 45 executive agencies, and it provides oversight and/or operation of 57 executive commissions, councils, and boards. The Idaho government is the largest employer in the state. Idahoans demand and deserve accountability, collaboration, and support for entrepreneurial activity within our departments. To ensure that by 2013 every state agency will provide to its customers—the children, families, and businesses of Idaho—the high-quality, effective, efficient, safe, and accountable services to which they are entitled, we must:

- Contain costs through increased public/private and nonprofit collaboration.
- Provide support within state agencies for improving service efficiency and effectiveness.
- Mobilize the untapped reserves of expertise and knowledge within our state to analyze, create, and implement streamlined state services.

Targeted Voters

As a first approximation, the counties of Idaho may be grouped by the generalized political character of their voters as follows:

- *Counties with a high percentage of voters who are anti-incumbent and Democratic-leaning independents but not yet ready to vote for an independent candidate:*

  - Ada
  - Bannock
  - Clearwater
  - Nez Perce
  - Latah
  - Blaine
  - Shoshone
  - Teton
  - Valley

- *Counties with a high number of voters who are a mixture of Democrats and Republicans:*

  - Kootenai
  - Bonneville
  - Twin Falls
  - Bonner
  - Bingham
  - Idaho
  - Elmore
  - Payette
  - Gem
  - Minidoka
  - Franklin

- *Counties with a low number of voters who are a mixture of Democrats and Republicans:*

  - Gooding
  - Boundary
  - Jerome
  - Washington
  - Lemhi

- *Counties with a high number of voters who are anti-incumbent and Republican-leaning, but a hard sell for an independent candidate:*

  - Canyon
  - Madison
  - Jefferson
  - Cassia
  - Fremont

Strategies and Tactics

Get on the Ballot

Collect 1,500+ signatures of registered voters on the voting ballot petitions for submission during the March filing period, using the following means:

- Identify and attend community events with large numbers of attendees, i.e., county fairs, tailgate parties, expos, tradeshows, etc.

- Recruit house party/signature event hosts from candidate friends, previous supporters, friends of friends, professional networks, campaign volunteers, etc.

- Generate media buzz/stories via blogs on current affairs, executive branch decisions/actions.

- Build social media contacts and utilize Facebook friends and Twitter fans to invite/guide people to community events to sign the petition and learn about the campaign.

- Utilize website for signature-gathering and pointing people to events/ volunteers/email for information on how to sign the petition.

Win

Garner 250,000 votes on 11/02/2010.

- Create name recognition and awareness statewide by the following means:
  - Utilize social media (Facebook friends, Twitter fans, blogging) with weekly communication.
  - Get interested people to the website.
  - Email updates monthly, then weekly June–October.
  - Research, schedule, and participate in speaking engagements, and attend community events.
  - Develop, produce, and implement video productions for YouTube, website, and PSAs/campaign advertising.

- Determine and implement paid advertising content and schedule.

- Determine and implement direct mail targets, content and schedule (minimum of three during May/June and three during September/ October).

- Develop and implement public relations/media relations contacts and stories.

- Conduct press conferences/media releases.

- January 14: Press conference to announce candidacy.

- May: Primary election reaction/commentary. Be available for photo opportunities and interviews.

- Participate in candidate debates.

- Research and identify community campaign/non profit PSA opportunities.

- Build a network of community/neighborhood advocates in targeted counties.

  - Recruit captains/team leaders in primary neighborhoods and cities in each targeted area or county.

  - Work with volunteers to secure sign placement in yards and other visible locations, coordination of house parties and other speaking venues, and getting out the vote (phone calls, door hangers).

- Develop a base of contributors that will generate the minimum $750,000 needed in in-kind and cash contributions, employing the following means:

  - Recruit prominent fundraising chairs.

  - Recruit contributions from base of previous supporters, new contacts/petition signers, Facebook friends, and email contacts.

  - Solicit contributions at all hosted signature parties/events.

  - Identify and recruit contributions pre-primary and post-primary.

  - Identify and recruit PAC contributions pre-primary and post-primary.

  - Work upgrades of contributions post-primary.

Our contribution goals are:

Number of Contributors	Contribution Amounts	Total Generated	% of Total
50	$5,000	$250,000	33%
150	$1,000	$150,000	20%
200	$ 500	$100,000	14%
5,000+	$50 or less	$250,000	33%
5,500		$750,000	100%

Personnel Needed

- Treasurer
- Campaign co-chairs (Prefer a male/female team to appeal to all demographics. Might be a husband/wife team, but doesn't have to be.)
- Campaign manager
- Campaign fundraising chair
- Volunteers for the core campaign team
- Volunteers statewide
- Contract labor for tasks and positions we are unable to staff with volunteers
- Other items to be determined

Campaign Tone

The tone for the campaign is one of integrity, reflecting the candidate's core value of serving the public interest rather than private or partisan expediency. This campaign renounces and condemns all mudslinging tactics. All campaign communications will be filtered through the question: "Would it serve the public interest to communicate this fact or message?" Damaging facts, stories, innuendos, and outright falsehoods will come out into the open independently of our campaign. Let's run our own race and operate with complete integrity.

Create a Campaign Calendar

Campaign calendars are critical to managing the work of campaign team members and volunteers. Be sure to maintain daily, weekly and monthly calendars. Share them with your family and campaign team so that everyone knows what is coming, where you'll be, and what support you'll need at each event. We found that using an online calendar worked well. You might also include, as we did, a roadtrip schedule for when you will reach out to specific groups, neighborhoods, cities or towns. Group your trips in such a way as to maximize your time and minimize your expenses.

Depending on the size and scope of your race, your campaign calendar may begin anywhere from four months to two years before election day. Begin scheduling as soon as your plan is drafted. Jump into the race and work hard no matter how many months are left in your race. Sometimes the last one in is the winner.

Lay your master calendar on a foundation of key filing dates, reporting deadlines, and major community events where you must appear in order to reach voters. Key dates include those related to balloting: signature submissions to county clerks and election offices, signature verifications, and count confirmations. Refine your calendar with tentative dates for campaign-initiated meet-the-candidate and fundraising events. Then overlay a timeline for the rollout of your campaign's media placements, including social media and web-based communications such as email, newsletter, and press release blasts. Overlay other timelines for recruiting supporters, volunteers, and contributors.

Speaking of contributions, event hosts avail themselves in order to help you raise funds. So keep track of who has committed to holding a meet-the-candidate/fundraising event for you. Cover as many areas of your election district as you can to reach the voters from whom you need to earn votes. Work these event dates into your master calendar.

As a sample of a master calendar, I offer you the following twenty-month calendar of key actions, events, and goals from my gubernatorial campaign. The closer your campaign comes to election day, the more critical it will be for you to have day-by-day and hour-by-hour calendars for yourself, your campaign team, and your volunteers.

SAMPLE MASTER CALENDAR

May 2009

- Secure campaign treasurer and file with election office.

- Secure a campaign manager.

June 2009

- Ready the campaign website with key features and content and a secure system for soliciting and receiving online contributions.

- Prepare for media coverage of candidacy.

July 2009

- Amend filing with election office to indicate seat for which candidate is running.

- Refine campaign website.

- Begin collecting 1,000 registered-voter, county election office-verified signatures to get onto the ballot.

- Send mailing to past campaign contributors to share the current candidacy news and to request financial support.

August 2009

- Research and populate databases for potential volunteers, contributors, and voters.

- Establish branded social media presences.

- Continue collecting signatures to get onto the ballot.

September 2009

- Attend events to share candidacy information.

- Continue collecting signatures to get onto the ballot.

October 2009

- Attend events to share candidacy information.

- Continue collecting signatures to get onto the ballot.

November 2009

- Attend events to share candidacy information.

- Continue collecting signatures to get onto the ballot.

December 2009

- Perform data entry for fundraising.
- Plan and budget.
- Secure information management chair.
- Update website.
- Continue collecting signatures to get onto the ballot.
- Prepare for press conferences.

January 2010

- Hold January 5th press conference to officially announce candidacy.
- Schedule speaking engagements for the year.
- Begin email newsletter.
- Identify and meet with targeted donors.

February 2010

- Continue email newsletter.
- Identify and meet with targeted donors.
- Hit the road; travel to targeted locations to meet voters.
- Get in touch with personal contacts for quiet support from people candidate knows.
- Reach new contacts; reach and strengthen social media outreach.

March 2010

- Continue email newsletter.
- Identify and meet with targeted donors.
- Hit the road. Reach new contacts; reach and strengthen social media outreach. File with the elections office to secure spot on the general election ballot.

April 2010

- Continue email newsletter.
- Identify and meet with high-quality targeted donors.
- Hit the road. Reach new contacts; reach and strengthen social media outreach. Media, media, media: get contacts, build lists, and reach out.

May 2010

- Continue email newsletter.
- Identify and meet with targeted donors.
- Hit the road. Reach new contacts; reach and strengthen social media outreach. Media, media, media: get contacts, build lists, and reach out.
- Participate in trade shows.

June 2010

- Continue email newsletter.
- Identify and meet with targeted donors.
- Hit the road. Reach new contacts; reach and strengthen social media outreach. Media, media, media: get contacts, build lists, and reach out.
- March in parades.
- Deliver flyers door-to-door by candidate and volunteers.
- Make city tours and deliver flyers.

July 2010

- Continue email newsletter.
- Identify and meet with targeted donors.
- Hit the road. Reach new contacts; reach and strengthen social media outreach. Media, media, media: get contacts, build lists, and reach out.
- March in parades.
- Deliver flyers door-to-door by candidate and volunteers.
- Make city tours and deliver flyers.

August 2010

- Continue email newsletter.
- Identify and meet with targeted donors.
- Hit the road. Reach new contacts; reach and strengthen social media outreach. Media, media, media: get contacts, build lists, and reach out.
- March in parades.
- Deliver flyers door-to-door by candidate and volunteers.
- Make city tours and deliver flyers.

- Staff fair booths.
- Respond to candidate surveys.

September 2010

- Continue email newsletter.
- Identify and meet with targeted donors.
- Hit the road. Reach new contacts; reach and strengthen social media outreach. Media, media, media: get contacts, build lists, and reach out.
- March in parades.
- Deliver flyers door-to-door by candidate and volunteers.
- Make city tours and deliver flyers.
- Staff fair booths.
- Attend candidate forums.
- Respond to candidate surveys.

October 2010

- Continue email newsletter.
- Identify and meet with targeted donors.
- Hit the road. Reach new contacts; reach and strengthen social media outreach. Media, media, media: get contacts, build lists, and reach out.
- Deliver yard signs. Idaho law is signs are not to go up more than thirty days before the election date.
- Deliver flyers door-to-door by candidate and volunteers.
- Respond to candidate surveys.
- Attend candidate forums.
- Participate in debates, in person and on television.

November 2010

- November 2, 2010 is election day. Hold an election night party for supporters.
- Close out the campaign, whatever the election results bring.

December 2010

- File final campaign report with election office.

Note Additional scheduling tips:

To meet enough people to earn a win, plan on two to four good events each day or on doing door-to-door campaigning all day.

Have your campaign manager involved in managing your calendar so that you get to the events and activities that help you reach your voters.

The bigger your campaign, the more you'll want to have a calendar keeper or scheduler to work with your campaign manager.

For local campaigns, you and your campaign manager can handle your calendar.

Campaign Manager Tasks

Your campaign manager, whether paid or volunteer, should know more about you and your campaign platform than anybody else but you. He or she must know even more than you do about the most effective ways to get you in front of your likeliest voters, contributors, and media outlets. Without a campaign manager, your campaign falters. You have plenty to do as the candidate and will need someone else to manage the work of getting you elected.

You will want to have detailed discussions with your campaign manager to reach agreement upon what he will and will not do for you and your campaign. Key tasks which a candidate generally delegates to her campaign manager include the following:

- Managing and coordinating all projects, tasks, and activities relating to getting you elected, beginning six months to two years before the date of the general election, depending on the office sought.

- Creating and managing the calendar of activities and events.

- Providing advice and insight to the candidate on marketing messages, campaign content and structure, places to appear in person, people to contact, monies to pursue and accept, places to advertise, and more.

- Overseeing and managing the campaign database, preferably in collaboration with a separate information management chair, as you'll see in the next section of this chapter.

- Creating and managing campaign meeting agendas.

- Managing and overseeing the campaign committee chairs and their tasks.

- Working collaboratively with the candidate, treasurer, campaign chairs, and committee chairs.

- Providing recommendations as requested while remembering that the candidate makes the final call on all decisions.

Fill Out the Rest of Your Campaign Team

Organizing the people who are working on a campaign is similar to constructing an organizational chart. In fact, I found that creating an organizational chart helped me to delegate, to manage projects, and to remember all of the functions and activities that needed to be addressed in order to have a successful campaign. The bigger the election district and the bigger the job of the elected seat, the more likely you'll need to have all of these campaign team members. The more local your race is, you may find that filling key positions one through five will be sufficient for managing the campaign.

Here are the key positions involved in running and managing a campaign.

1. *Candidate*: You are the owner of the company, the chairman of the board, and the candidate. All decisions stop with you. The way you manage your team is the way your team will interact in the community during the process of campaigning.

2. *Campaign Treasurer*: See Chapter 5.

3. *Campaign Manager*: See this chapter.

4. *Campaign Chair or Co-Chairs*: The bigger your campaign's territorial reach and the bigger the dollar amount you need to raise, the more helpful it becomes to have campaign chairs. These are the high-profile, well-known people whom voters trust and who can help you earn votes simply because their name(s) are on your letterhead and fundraising requests.

5. *Fundraising Chair*: This is the person who does the work and manages the committee to raise funds. In really large campaigns, this is a high-profile figurehead who is supported by a do-the-work committee chair and committee. More on this in Chapter 8.

6. *Messaging/Marketing/Advertising Director*: You decide what to call this job. This person keeps your message consistent and works with a

committee to get the word out about you in as many places as possible to earn you the votes you need.

7. *Information Management Director*: Every campaign needs a database of voters, donors, event hosts, volunteers, and contacts. Having a computer/software expert on your team is critical to your success because so much of campaigning is now dependent on computers.

8. *Office Manager*: Depending on the size of your campaign, you may have an administrative position that literally manages an office. None of my campaigns had need of this position because we ran each campaign out of our houses rather than spending money on an office.

9. *Committees*: You and your campaign manager will find it valuable to set up campaign committees. You may choose from among the following categories and recruit one person or a team, depending on the size and scope of your race:

    ▪ *Fundraising Events*: This committee works with the fundraising chair to conduct events that raise money for the campaign.

    ▪ *Campaign Advisory*: These individuals may work publicly or behind the scenes to give you advice about what is happening in your race and what is happening in the geographic area affected by your race. These individuals may know each other, or they may not. You can work with them individually or call them together for meetings—whatever they are willing to do to support and advise your campaign.

    ▪ *Policy Advisory and Candidate Survey Review*: This team includes subject matter experts who can help you create policy statements and white papers, which are three to hundreds of pages long and describe what you know about a specific topic or a range of topics, and what you intend to do when elected. This team also reviews candidate surveys that you fill out—before you return them to the requesting groups. In some cases the team may advise, "Don't respond."

    ▪ *Research and Policy*: This team helps track down data, statistics, current affairs, hot topic details, key people, and competing candidate information. And then it shares the digested information with you so you stay current and informed.

- *Candidate Events*: This team works with your calendar keeper and fundraising chair to be sure you are seen and heard in the right places to earn votes.

- *Press Conference*: This team schedules the times, places, and topics of your press conferences and gets the media to attend and report them.

- *Debate and Forum Preparation*: This team helps you refine and rehearse your public-speaking skills, both set speeches and improvisational exchanges.

- *Newsletters/Email*: This team develops, edits, and distributes your communications in hardcopy and email formats in conformity with the overall messaging of the campaign.

- *Website*: This team makes sure that the website is current and may be the liaison with your technical person, or may in fact be the technical person managing the site.

- *Social Media/Blogs*: If you don't post yourself, have someone you trust with your life and your image do the posting. Stay consistent with the tone and messaging of your campaign.

- *Collateral Material Production*: Flyers, door hangers, mailings, bumper stickers, pencils, buttons, and anything that gets your name in front of people via a hold-in-your-hand item fits into this committee's work. You want a team with an eye for clear messaging, for details, and for branding consistency. You are the brand!

- *Marketing*: Letters to the editor, content creation for use in collateral materials and advertisements, any articles written about you, and working with the related committees to provide the content and messaging they need is the task of this committee.

- *Advertising*: This team researches or proposes print, radio, television and online advertising possibilities. It creates and proposes budgets. It organizes and makes advertising buys.

- *Video Production*: Find a chair who understands video for online and television uses. Hire or recruit a really good team.

- *Parades, Fairs, and Trade Shows*: This person or committee coordinates calendars, enters the float/unit in parades, and recruits volunteers to walk with you or work a booth with you. Have a team member compile what is happening in your election district so you can add events to your calendar. For example, we participated in over a dozen parades, three regional state fairs (Idaho doesn't have one state fair), and in four tradeshows and gunshows. Be sure to track the number of people in attendance at each event so that you can measure your outreach.

- *Volunteer Coordination*: The bigger your election district, the more likely you'll need volunteer coordinators to support the campaign manager in completing tasks and staffing events.

- *Endorser and Supporter Recruitment*: This person gets permission to use names in literature and advertisements from people who are supporting you and your campaign. Important: Use a person's name and endorsement only when you secure formal written permission.

- *Special Audience*: This committee will help you meet with the groups of targeted voters you know you must reach, such as the following:

  - Law enforcement officers

  - Teachers

  - Business community members

  - State employees

  - City/county/parish employees and employee unions

  - District employees

  - Gun owners

  - Constitution supporters

  - Environmental and land-use advocates

  - Animal advocates

  - Child advocates

  - Labor unions

▨ **Note** Volunteers are the lifeblood of your campaign. They'll spread the word. They'll be your arms and legs for getting things done. They'll be your friends when you celebrate the campaign on election night. Recruit as many volunteers as you can to accomplish meaningful work.

Find Volunteers

The saying—"If you don't ask, you don't get"—applies to recruiting volunteers. People rarely volunteer themselves for political campaigns. Typically, you must ask for, invite, and even cajole people to volunteer in small and big ways on your campaign. Volunteers are the lifeblood of your campaign. Volunteers can provide one thing or accomplish hundreds of tasks for your campaign. Volunteers come on board because they believe in you, want to help, want to learn something about campaigning, and want to have fun too. Every once in awhile, someone who volunteers for your campaign is really a mole, or spy (for another candidate), so evaluate critically the reasons people give for volunteering. Ask questions such as, "What other campaigns have you worked on?" Read body language to determine sincerity and suitability.

You may find that five to ten volunteers can accomplish everything outlined in this chapter in order for your campaign to win. Or you may discover that you need hundreds of volunteers to reach the minimum number of voters who need to hear about you and to vote for you. Regardless of how many volunteers you discover you need, clear communication skills and tools are needed for successful campaign and volunteer management.

Volunteers can best be managed by you and your campaign manager. Volunteers want you to be present. In fact, during my 2010 race, some party-supporters defected to my independent campaign because they saw me showing up at events, while their party-affiliated guy was promising to attend the same events but not actually showing up. Volunteers also want to feel noticed, acknowledged, and appreciated by you, so show up and share the love. Your campaign manager can handle the tasks to be accomplished by volunteers.

▨ **Note** Project management tools and clear communication keep your staff and volunteers on task, on time, and on budget.

No Campaign Plan? Plan to Lose Your Race

If at this point you are thinking, "Oh, I'll just wing it," your chances of winning are somewhere between zero and nil. Winning an elected office position requires greater diligence than applying for a job in an organization or company in which you may interview with one to twenty individuals. Why? Because running for office requires you to secure hundreds, thousands, hundreds of thousands, or even millions of votes. Without a plan to reach the myriads of people who need to know who you are, you will have difficulty organizing your time. Without a campaign plan, you may find yourself tempted to spend money on every campaign offer that comes your way (you'll be surprised at the onslaught of mail you receive about buying campaign items). Without a campaign plan you will be more likely to react to what is happening in your race than to be in control of your message and your time so that you can tell your story and get yourself elected.

With a campaign plan, you will be able to keep your and your team's focus on the race you are running. With a campaign plan, you can stay on track and on budget. With a campaign plan in hand, you are more likely to attract contributions and volunteers and to earn votes.

Conclusion

Your campaign plan is a living document and a document to live by. It's your ongoing project management tool for each day's activity and every task you and your campaign manager delegate. With your campaign plan in hand, you are positioned to create and deliver your campaign messages in ways and in places where you can get heard and recognized as the right person for voters to cast their ballots. Your campaign plan is the roadmap to victory.

Run: Hone Your Message

You've officially begun your campaign because you have filed to run and have formulated your campaign plan. Now for your message. It's time to go public with the message of why are you running. Your message will include not only why you are running but also what you intend to do once in office.

You may find, as I did, that telling your story in a way that inspires others to vote for you is challenging. This is why you have formed a campaign message team. This team will help you to identify your base voters and the messages that will best reach them. Each message statement you craft must be true to who you are and what you intend to do. Each message statement can be re-stated in a variety of ways to reach the voters you want to reach. Read the following examples to see how a commitment to education may be framed differently, yet stated truthfully, in order to reach different voters:

- *I support education*: Few people would disagree with such a big catch-all statement, but most people would also wonder, "Where's the beef?" So, be prepared to share some specifics.

- *I support educational choice*: Some people, the ones who care about school choice, will know what this means. The phrase means you believe that public schools, private schools, home schooling, magnet and charter schools are all viable school options that should be eligible for public funding. If you don't believe this, then don't say it.

- *I support the proper funding of education*: Voters will naturally ask whether you mean *more* or *less* funding. My standard response to this was: "I don't think we know what the proper amount of funding is because the research needs to be done to tell us what a reasonable dollar amount of funding really is." Although this response might seem like ducking the question, in Idaho the research truly has not been done to establish what a proper dollar amount for funding education should be year over year.

- *I support pre-K and K-12 education*: The message here is that you believe in public funding for pre-kindergarten as well as kindergarten through twelfth grade education. Many in Idaho believe that pre-kindergarten education should not be publicly funded.

- *I support K-12 and higher education*: The message here is that you believe in public funding for post-secondary as well as kindergarten through twelfth grade education. Many in Idaho believe that post-secondary education should not be publicly funded.

- *I support twenty-first century preparation of teachers so that they can provide world-class education for twenty-first century students*: Be prepared to flesh out your message: "Today's students learn in different ways than the students of the last century. Teachers need to be prepared to meet today's students' Web 2.0 learning styles and educational needs. Our institutions of higher education must adapt their teacher training methods and courses to prepare teachers for the students of this century."

For every statement you speak in public or publish in your literature, have supporting information about what you believe and why, as well as supporting action items that you will pursue when elected.

What's Your Platform?

Your platform is essentially a list of your political values, together with the political actions you will take to promote those same values if you are elected. For maximum effect, platform values and actions are stated in pithy bullet points that are recognized and valued by your targeted voters. Following are some random examples:

Platform Values

- Family values
- Pro-life
- Pro-choice
- The First Amendment defends all the rest
- The Second Amendment defends all the rest
- Constitutional originalism
- No new taxes
- Energy independence
- Protect our public resources and lands from corporate greed
- Preserve our public resources for corporate good
- Early childhood education is a parental prerogative
- America for Americans

Platform Actions

- Stop the XL Keystone Pipeline
- Drill here, drill now
- Seal our borders now
- Provide safe routes to school and safe school zones
- Fund early childhood education
- Create more jobs
- Clean up our city
- Improve our roads
- Cap property taxes
- Build a new jail/police station/bridge/park/fire station
- Reform mandatory sentencing laws
- Fund emergency services
- Flatten the tax code

- Close tax loopholes for billionaires
- Stop stealth socialism
- End corporate socialism

Platform values often conjure up opposite sets of associated meanings, depending on whether the candidate's platform is conservative or liberal. Consider the first example, "family values."

In a conservative platform, "family values" is associated with opposition to sex outside of traditional marriage, whether premarital sex, adultery, polygamy, nonmarital cohabitation, incest, bestiality, group sex, or homosexual sex; opposition to same-sex marriage; opposition to egalitarian aspects of feminism and support of Bible-based complementarian roles between husband and wife; support for enabling parents to exercise full control of their children's education, including public vouchers for private, faith-based, and home K-12 schooling; opposition to abortion and support for premarital abstinence and extramarital adoption; support of abstinence education and opposition to sex education; opposition to pornography, obscenity, and depictions of sexuality in the media; and opposition to the separation of church and state.

In a liberal platform, the same term "family values" is associated with a quite different set of meanings: support of a living wage, universal health care, sex education, and social and financial assistance for working families, including family planning, child care, and maternity leave; and egalitarian acceptance of non-traditional families, including those headed by single parents and same-sex adoptive parents.

Define your platform clearly so that you and everyone on your campaign team knows what each of your platform statements means. As you've just read, the same "family values" phrase can lead people to drastically different conclusions about who you are, what you stand for, and what you plan to do.

What Do You Want to See Changed?

Part of your message to voters is to share what you want to see changed. Be specific. "Taxes" is not a useful response. Do you want to see more taxes collected to pay for needed services, or do you want to see taxes lowered to inspire job creation? "Protect the environment" is not a sound answer because it does not communicate what you want to see happen. Will you oppose drilling, logging, and mining? Or will you support them?

Provide enough specifics that voters can picture themselves benefitting from the changes you propose.

For example, Mothers Against Drunk Drivers (MADD) formed because of their anger over the loss of children and family members to drunken driver-caused accidents. As a group, they wanted laws to become more harsh to punish people who drink, drive, and cause harm. As a group, they succeeded in getting heard, providing education, changing laws, and changing societal attitudes about drunken driving.

Another grassroots example of the success of specific and passionate messaging is the spectacular rise of the Tea Party movement across the United States in 2009. A loose affiliation of like-minded local groups, Tea Partiers are against taxes, against raising taxes, in favor of small government and strict adherence to the U.S. Constitution, and fed up with business as usual in Washington and their state capitals. The number of Tea Party activists and sympathizers quickly became such a large and energetic part of the Republican base that they affected election outcomes at national and state levels in the 2010 election cycle and are again shaping the GOP field and platforms in the primary phase of the 2012 cycle. An even more recent example of outraged and disgusted citizens rising up in protest of the status quo are the Occupy Wall Street occupations of public areas in cities across the nation, in protest of widening wealth, power, and opportunity disparities.

Building on the list of ideas you've already drafted in Chapter 2 about what you want to see changed, create clear statements about what you intend to do if elected. You are running for office because you want to do something that you feel others have not accomplished, or because you want to nudge the organizational entity for which you are running to change course. Have your message team review your statements for clarity, consistency, and passion. Ask them to suggest language that will resonate positively with your most likely voters. Conversely, ask them to flag language whose unintended meanings might turn your voters off.

Who's Your Base Voter?

You know who you are and why you are running. Your challenge is to find the people who care about what you care about and figure out whether there are enough of them to get you elected. If you conclude that your core base of voters isn't big enough to get you elected, then you've got broaden your base by reaching out to a larger group of base voters. Your goal is to communicate clearly, gain name recognition, and earn enough votes to win.

Conduct research to pinpoint your potential voters. To win, you will need more than the people who already know you to vote for you. Explore each of the following possibilities:

- *People who have voted before in this race*: Election offices have this information and can prepare voter lists that tell you who has voted in the last several elections for this particular office and where they live.

- *People who care about your issues and platforms*: These are the topics important to you and a part of your campaign. Revisit Chapter 2.

- *Groups that care about what you are focused upon and what you want to do*: Ask for an opportunity to make presentations to these groups and to field questions from their members.

- *People who voted for your party in past races*: Political parties keep lists of voters, donors, and likely voters. Build a relationship with your chosen political party so that you can earn access to their voter lists. In most cases, the parties can help prepare door-to-door lists, mailing lists, and volunteer lists.

- *People who voted for the incumbent and are unhappy*: This is harder to uncover in a list format. Identification of this group comes from reading and listening to community reports about which individuals and which industry groups are unhappy with the incumbent.

- *People new to voting*: Some candidates actively pursue those who are new to voting: high school students, newly naturalized citizens, newly registered voters, and so on. Some candidates pinpoint civic groups that seem to be newly engaged in gathering candidate information. Still other candidates pursue people new to the election district. These new voters are often challenging to pinpoint.

- *Absentee voters*: As a candidate, you can request the absentee voter list that the election office produces during the days before the election date, sometimes daily.

Next, you must identify how to reach these voters. Determine whether you'll share the same message with every group, or whether you will adapt your message to each group while remaining truthful. Research the following questions concerning outreach venues, modes, and channels:

- *Where do they live?* Use mailing lists or door-to-door walk lists to pinpoint where to deliver flyers and mailings.

- *Where do they hang out or gather?* Consider using flyers, bumper stickers, and posters in specific locations as tools to tell your story.

- *Where do they work and eat lunch?* Discover whether workplaces host meet-the-candidate events. Some do, many don't. Have flyers, posters, bus, subway and train signage, yard signs, and even billboards on walking, commuting, and driving routes to get your name and campaign in front of people.

- *What are their social hot-spots? Online? Listservs? Blogs? Face-to-face?* Find out where people gather so you can go there and meet people, virtually or in-person.

- *Who are the absentee voters?* Ask to get onto the election office's distribution list.

- *Where do your likely voters go for religious services?* Some religious groups and service-holders host meet-the-candidate forums.

- *Where do they get information?* Some trade groups, civic groups, and voter leagues host debates. Find out which groups will be hosting events and be sure to get your place in the debate or forum.

- *One week before Election Day, what will your messages be?* Determine whether your messages will stay the same, or whether you will need a changed message thread as the election draws to a close.

- *During the ballot mail-out and deadline-for-return period for states with mail-in balloting, what will your message be to reach these voters?* Determine what message or message sequence you will use in print, in advertisements, and in mailings to reach these voters.

Once you've identified whom to reach, you need to answer these questions to know where it would be most profitable to spend your outreach time. For instance, if you determine going door to door is a cost-effective form of outreach for you, you'll want to have some literature to leave behind.

- *Doorhangers:* These printed cards tell who you are, what you want to do in office, and how to find out more about you. Sometimes the cards are physically produced in such a way that they can be hung on doorknobs and door handles (Figure 7-1). Sometimes your literature can be bagged in a doorhanger sleeve big enough for multiple candidates' information inserts (Figure 7-2).

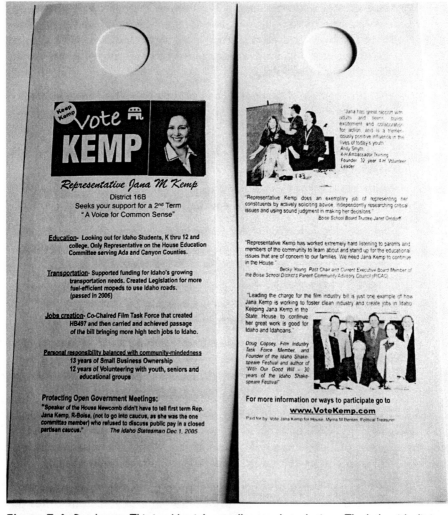

Figure 7-1. *Doorhanger.* This is a blue ink on yellow card stock piece. The hole with slit is used to hang the card over door knobs and handles. Beware, in the wind, these don't always stay put.

Figure 7-2. *Bagged doorhanger.* In some cases, bundling your literature with other office-seekers gives you more power. Bundling literature requires a great deal of volunteer coordination to get the bags put together and then to get them delivered. The plastic bag can protect literature from the weather.

- *Flyers*: Candidate flyers (Figures 7-3 and 7-4) are another viable format for leave-behinds. They too tell who you are and what you plan to do in office, as well as providing contact information such as your campaign website.

Figure 7-3. *Four-color postcard mailer.* Postcards can be mailed and be used as in-person give-away cards. Four-color cards tend to be more eye-catching than one-color cards. This card was a reminder to vote on Election Day.

Figure 7-4. *Four-color information card.* This candidate information card was produced after a newspaper endorsement and delivered by hand to voter addresses.

- *Business Cards*: These are the smallest and least expensive campaign pieces to print. Yet they provide a way for people to remember your name and to find out more on your website or social media pages (Figure 9-1).

These are just a few examples from my campaigns. Many more are depicted in Chapter 9, and also online in color at www.JanaKemp.com/RunForOffice.

Be Honest

On several occasions, I found myself candidly saying to people, "If being anti-abortion is your number-one decision criterion for casting your vote, then Mr. Pro-Life is the only candidate in the race who matches your value set. If you have concerns across a variety of issues, then I invite you to check me and my candidacy out because I'd like to earn your vote." Some people thanked me for my honesty and voted for him. Others thanked me, said they would cast their vote based upon many factors, and then took more time to learn about me. Still others, not hearing what they had wanted to hear, would simply turn and walk away.

Telling people what they want to hear when it is not what you believe or what you will do is a lie. While serving as a state representative, I saw and heard a senator say one thing to a group in the morning and the exact opposite to an education group in the afternoon. Had I not seen and heard it myself, I would not have believed it. Don't do this. At every level of elected and non-elected office we need honest people. Honesty does not require brutally expressing your opinions. There is a big difference between saying, "My kids are out of school—schools don't need more money!" and saying, "We need to take a serious look at whether schools are receiving too much funding." The first statement may be how you feel, yet the second statement is a more objective and less offensive way of saying that school funding needs to be reviewed.

Honesty also does not require that you pull up a chair and share every bit of information that you hold. First and foremost, people want to know that you understand their concerns. Then people want to know that you know enough to do the job, that you will be careful and caring when making decisions, or that you are likeable enough that they'll vote for you.

Publishing Position Pieces

Some voters and contributors will ask to see in-depth essays, white papers, or position pieces that detail what you believe, what you plan to do, and whom you will enlist to help you accomplish your campaign pledges. They'll ask for these documents to learn more about what you believe, who you are, and to determine whether they will support you. Taking time to document in detail what you believe and plan to do for each of your platform items is worthwhile.

Beware, however, of people who ask for position papers on every possible topic involved in an election. You do not have time to do this. Stay focused on your main messages. Determine whether a requested white paper is really worth your time and will really garner you financial support equal to the time you put into the effort. I've found that some people will ask for details and still won't write a contribution check. So, why lose time that you could be spending with people who will contribute and will vote for you? Don't. Winning is about the numbers: about the number of people you can reach and encourage to vote for you. You need to get your message out to as many potential voters as possible.

Post your key position statements online and direct people to your website for details. Tweet how to find the details of your positions. Link your social media pages to your website. Your campaign website should be the home of detailed position statements and campaign platforms.

Also know that the more you publish about your positions, the more content your competition has to use to create their positions and to use your own words against you during media events, debates, and in print. Do it anyway. Share what your positions are, because voters want to know.

Candidate Surveys

Refining your message is important for your campaign pieces and for crafting the language of your responses to candidate surveys. Many organizations reach out to their members and encourage them to vote based on candidate responses to group-specific questionnaires and surveys. The National Rifle Association sends out surveys. Local chapters of chambers of commerce, environmental groups, and churches as well as other value-focused groups send out candidate surveys.

Two examples of candidate surveys follow. The first is from the state K-12 teachers union, the Idaho Education Association (IEA). To give you an idea of the highly specific kinds of questions you'll be asked by some interest groups, I've paraphrased the IEA survey questions, which were very long and technical, and given verbatim a few of my responses:

IDAHO EDUCATION ASSOCIATION QUESTIONNAIRE: OFFICE OF GOVERNOR

March 2010

1. Three-part question about funding levels for K-12 schools and changing the super-majority for bond passage to a simple majority.

2. Reduce student classroom size to no more than 20 students per classroom. Agree or disagree and why.

3. Staff development, student remediation, testing question.

4. IEA wants the Annual Contract Support Program reinstated and funded. Agree or disagree.

5. $40,000 beginning teacher salary. Agree or disagree.

6. Get Idaho average salary to U.S. Teacher's average salary. Agree or disagree.

7. Public funds for public schools. Agree or disagree.

    Agree. A free public education is provided for in Idaho's constitution and must be protected and provided for as such. Private education (schools and home-schooling) is an opt-in choice and should be protected as an ongoing choice for the families who choose to pursue non-public education and non-public funding.

8. Alternative pay systems (such as merit-based pay for teachers), which IEA opposes. Agree or disagree.

9. Continue funding teachers achieving National Board Certification.

10. Don't change the PERSI system (state's retirement plan) for teachers and other education professionals. Agree or disagree.

11. Don't change the due process for renewable-contract teachers. Agree or disagree.

12. Support & Protect our Support Professionals. Agree or disagree.

    Agree. The implication of this question is that this is not the process now. How many people would this legislation protect? How many have had problems over the last ten years on this front? (Note: I answered with questions to invite the association to stay in conversation with me, to continue providing information to me, and to be engaged in collaborative problem solving in the future.

13. As governor, will you welcome IEA as a partner?

14. Will you ensure students are the sole beneficiaries of state lands?

15. Discuss your commitment to managing school trust lands and investments from them.

16. How will you use your position as governor to advocate for public schools?

17. What will you do to address the coming teacher shortage?

    Work with the executive agencies, Board and Department of Education as well as the legislature to establish rules and laws that will:

    - Inspire people to become teachers.

    - Incentivize Idaho's best and brightest people to choose teaching for their second or third careers.

    - Incentivize Idaho's best and brightest people to become first-time teachers in all subject areas. Trying to pay K-12 teachers of one subject a higher salary than those who teach another fails, in my opinion, to recognize that ALL skill sets and subject matter are of equal value to student development!

    - Work with Idaho's universities and colleges to create teacher training for the twenty-first century, so that people who graduate with K-8 and 9-12 certifications will be prepared to stay and feel confident about staying in the teaching and school administration and related student-service professions, all the while being able to meet the learning and disciplinary needs of twenty-first century students. I'd love to see Idaho once again have on-campus lab-schools for pioneering of twenty-first century teaching, inspiring and disciplining models that will lead students to ever-better lives and life-long problem-solving and learning.

18. As governor, what will you do to help challenged students achieve academic success?

19. If money is still tight by January 2011, what would you recommend to ensure adequate funding of schools?

20. As governor, what would be your top three priorities for Idaho public schools?

Thank You! Thank you so much for inviting me to the discussion table. I look forward to working with you as we all work for Idaho's future.

The second sample candidate survey is from a metropolitan daily newspaper, the *Idaho Statesman*. The *Statesman* published a summary of candidate responses in its newspaper a week before the election and posted the candidates' full responses on its website. The questions are typical of those you'll see in candidate surveys by newspapers and other mass media.

IDAHO STATESMAN QUESTIONS 2010

- Why are you running?

- What makes you a better choice for voters than your opponent(s)?

- What should voters know about you as a person?

- What living Idaho politician do you most respect, and why? (No dead people)

- What decision did you make during your adult life that you most regret, and how has it changed you?

- What are three things you want to accomplish first if elected (or re-elected)?

- What state law enacted in the past five years do you most disagree with, and why? What law enacted in that period do you most strongly support, and why?

- Four years from now, how should Idaho differ from today? What should your role be in achieving that change?

- Appropriations to Idaho public schools and universities took a significant cut in 2010. State rainy-day and federal economic-stimulus funds that have helped sustain education spending through the recession are largely spent. What should the Legislature do in 2011 about public school and higher-education budgets?

- Some state leaders want to cut individual and corporate income taxes, perhaps over 10 years. Should Idaho do this? Why or why not? If yes: By how much, and when?

- Should the state spend more to maintain and upgrade highways, as Gov. Butch Otter has urged? If yes: Where should Idaho get the money?

- Should the legislature give local governments the option of asking their citizens to approve sales tax increases that could pay for public transportation or other local needs? Why or why not?

- What, if anything, should the legislature do about illegal immigration?

- On an A through F scale, what grade would you assign the Idaho Legislature's work since the 2008 election, and why?

- On an A through F scale, what grade would you assign Gov. Butch Otter's work since he was elected in 2006, and why?

Ask your message team to review your responses. What you think is a clear response may not be. What you feel is a great response may be twisted and used against you. Be sure that you are being clear and consistent with your campaign platform and messages when responding to surveys and questionnaires. Over the years, inconsistencies have taken candidates out of contention in the middle of a race and during the final days approaching election day.

Issue Management

Issue management is primarily focused on keeping track of what you and your opponents are discussing so that you can clearly differentiate yourself from others in the race. You have your positions and concerns. Your opponents have theirs too. Be sure to keep a log of your comments on issues. Keep a log of community issues and concerns along with a log of your competitors' comments on issues. These logs of comments, position statements, news items, and facts are useful in conversation, speeches, candidate forums, and debates.

Some issues will be longstanding concerns of your community, district, and voters. Other issues—such as natural disasters, law changes from other places that stir up constituents in your district, or even human tragedies—may arise in the midst of the campaign. Be prepared to speak to both the longstanding issues and the topical issues that seem to come out of nowhere. Demonstrate your wide knowledge, thoughtful intelligence, and emotional care every time you are asked questions.

Be consistent in who you are and what you say. In these days of campaign trackers armed with video-enabled smart phones, telling one group one thing and another group a different thing will soon get you branded as a "waffler." This label won't win you any votes.

■ **Note** Only put in print or post online things that you believe and know to be true.

Framing Your Opponent(s)

How are you like your opponents? How are you subtly or dramatically different from your opponents? Maybe you are all men. Maybe you all belong to the same social clubs. Maybe you are all moving in different circles. Maybe you all hunt. Maybe none of you has ever held office before. Maybe you are all women. Maybe you are men and women wanting to serve the community in similar ways. How will you help yourself stand out? Maybe you are the only one with the experience and knowledge to do the job. Maybe you are the only one who has lived in your district for your whole life. Maybe you bring solutions that no one else is offering.

Framing your opponents is equally about framing both them and yourself. Framing is the act and process of telling stories and sharing platform statements in such a manner that voters can clearly picture you and why they want to vote for you and not for your opponents.

In a first-time run for office, your message is the only thing people have to go on to decide whether or not to vote for you. In a repeat run for office, your message reminds people of what you've done and asks people to vote for you so that you can keep doing the job. You have less of a need to comment on your opponents than they have to comment on you. They are trying to unseat you. You are trying to keep the seat that you hold. As a result, it is imperative for people to see, know, and feel the reasons that they should vote to return you to office.

Polling

Polling is a survey of prospective voters that is designed to give you information about who is likely to vote for you and what voter interests are. Polls enable you to reach voters with messages that mean something to them and will get them to vote for you. Polling is usually an expensive proposition for collecting data that has a short life of relevance.

Polling can help you pinpoint constituent concerns. Polling can also be helpful when you want to know people's opinions about you and your competitors so that you can begin to differentiate yourself from competitors. Polling these days really seems most used in and by the media, to help the media create stories about issues and candidates and what may, or may not, be happening in any given race.

Polling is of no use when you take a poll months before you plan to use the data, because a poll is a snapshot from the past. Week to week in a campaign, things can change, including opinions. Keeping your ear to the ground and your campaign team members focused on hearing what is happening day after day in the community gives you a better chance of learning what is truly important to voters.

If a polling company is trying to convince you to pay for them to conduct a poll, ask a lot of questions, such as:

- Whom do you poll? How do you create your lists? You want to know this because if the polling companies' lists are all from the opposite party, you will not get meaningful information about your most likely voters.

- How many people will you survey? The pollsters need to ask the opinions of at least 500 people, not just make 500 calls, to create a reasonable picture of a voting area's opinions. The bigger the election district, the more people who need to be contacted.

- Do I get to review the polling questions? If they say "no," get away from that company as quickly as possible—you are about to be taken for your cash. If they say yes—great! Have your message team review the questions with you.

- How much will it cost? Ask this question before committing to anything.

During my 2010 race for governor, neither the Democratic nor Republican candidates shared any of the results of the polls conducted on their behalf. They never made the traditional campaign move of turning their polling data into press releases and news stories because neither one was happy with what the polls were telling them. We saw the Republican incumbent work harder than he had worked in any previous election over the last two decades. We saw the Democratic candidate redouble his efforts, even attempting to persuade some of my campaign team members to defect.

Although polls can provide your campaign with useful information, never forget that they are snapshots of the past. In an election, you must focus on today and tomorrow in order to anticipate what people will feel is important on the day they cast their ballots.

No Campaign Message? Plan to Lose Your Race

People must know who you are, why you are running, and what you plan to do once elected. When voters do not know these key points about you, they tend to vote by party affiliation or name recognition. Continue to refine and control your message so that you can tell your story and get yourself elected. As the race unfolds, your campaign team's job is to make sure that every day more people have heard your name together with good reasons for casting their votes for you.

With a clear and consistent message you will be able to get voters to consider voting for you. Your message statements, position papers, issue comments, candidate survey responses, and plans for action together tell voters why they should vote for you.

Conclusion

Become so clear about your message that no one can pull you off course. Internalize your talking points so that you can tell your story any time, any place, to any audience, without having to refer to your notes. In a first-time run for office, your message is all that people have to go on to decide whether or not to vote for you. In a repeat run for office, your message reminds people what you've done, and asks people to vote for you again so that you can keep doing the job.

Run: Raise Money

Some races can be won for as little as a hundred dollars. However, most races require thousands or tens of thousands of dollars. National races require millions and sometimes billions of dollars to run and win. Think of running a campaign as starting a business. You have a plan and you have a message about the "product," which is you. You need money to work your plan to get voters to learn about you, and to cast their ballots for you so that you can win and do the job.

Money can come in the form of cash, check, or credit card contributions. Financial contributions can also come in the form of in-kind services or goods, which are items or services that the campaign does not have to pay for, but does have to record in financial reports. So, consider money and in-kind items as resources to ask for when fundraising.

Asking for campaign funds may or may not be a challenge for you as the candidate. If you have the personality of a salesperson, you may love this aspect of campaigning. Most of us who run for office find fundraising one of the most difficult tasks, because it is, after all, asking for money. Some candidates schedule regular days of the week to make fundraising phone calls. For big contributions, people really do want to be asked in person, rather than by mail. Some candidates rely on well-known people to do most of the fundraising, which only works if the well-known people are willing and able to do the work of political fundraising.

Note Without an adequate amount of money to get the word out to voters that you are in the race, you are destined to lose.

How Much Money Will It Take to Get the Word Out and Win?

First, determine what others have spent in recent races for this office. Ask your election office how to access financial reports of past campaigns. Look at the reports for the winners and losers of races in each of the last four election cycles to determine a budget amount for your campaign. Track the amounts spent and whether the person won or lost. This exercise will give you a reasonable dollar amount to target in your fundraising. Independent Minnesota Governor Jesse Ventura won his race in 1998 with about $400,000. Yet, in 2010, Republican Meg Whitman lost her race for governor of California after spending about $178 million dollars, which was over $140 million more than her winning Democrat challenger spent in the race.

I've discovered when talking to people about how much it costs to run for office that they are surprised how much gets spent in local elections. So, base your budget goal on the real numbers others have spent in the past. You may feel that you can spend less—and with wise spending, you may be right. You may, on the other hand, feel that you need to raise more than was raised in past races because the district has changed and you have more people to reach in order to get the vote count that you need to win.

In addition to studying how much money previous candidates have raised, study where the money was spent. Learning where others spent money will help you identify where to spend, and how to set your budget and spending limits. If you are running against an incumbent, review his or her past election reports to learn from whom money was received and where money was spent. You can learn where he or she is most likely to spend money to get re-elected, based on where money was spent in the past. For instance, you may discover that past candidates spent a lot of money on signs. Will you? Or will you create a different spending plan to achieve your win?

Your Treasurer Is Not Your Fundraising Chair

You selected your treasurer to help you with record keeping and reports. Most treasurers prefer to work behind the scenes on the details of tracking and reporting the funds coming into and going out of the campaign account. A fundraising chair, or fundraising co-chair, is responsible for getting the word out to people who can and will contribute to the campaign. The chair needs to meet people, make the "ask" on your behalf, and introduce you to people who will contribute to the campaign. The best fundraising chairs really do the work of generating money for your campaign. The worst fundraising chairs come along for the ride, enjoy the parties, and never ask for contributions.

Local campaigns as well as national campaigns benefit from having a fundraising chair. The bigger the race, the more necessary it is to have a fundraising chair who will work hard to gather contributions to the campaign. The bigger the race, the more you have to be free to work the campaign trail: meeting and talking with as many prospective voters and contributors at as many venues and events as you possibly can each day.

What to Look For in Your Fundraising Chair

Many times candidates will choose people who are well-known in the community, who have served in office before, or are great fun to be around. Add to the needed-qualities list for a fundraising chair someone who is prominent, credible, and able to ask for and get money. Remember, if people are not asked to give, ninety-nine percent of the time they will not give.

You will also want a fundraising chair who believes in you, your platform, and your chances of winning the race. Whomever you have asking for money has to be believed by the people being asked to part with their non-tax-deductible money. Political contributions are not tax-deductible. Check with an accountant in your state to be sure you and your campaign are clear about all of the rules of giving and receiving campaign contributions. Again, the best fundraising chairs do the work of generating money for your campaign so that you can focus on meeting people, answering questions, and earning votes.

Note The best fundraising chairs really do the work of generating money for your campaign.

Create a Budget and Stick to It

Begin your fundraising process by creating a budget. Whether your budget is for a local election that may only require several hundred dollars, and you plan to fund the race yourself, or your budget is tens of thousands of dollars that you'll need to raise from other people's contributions, you must have a budget. Identify where and how you plan to spend campaign money. Once you've pinpointed the amount of money you'll need, you can announce your fundraising goal. People want to know how much money you think you need to win and where you plan to spend their money.

One of our campaign rules in 2004, 2006, and 2010 was "don't spend it unless we have it in the bank." My rationale for this remains: "If you can't run a financially sound and responsible campaign, then why should voters put you in office to mishandle their money too?" Handle your campaign monies the way you plan to handle tax dollars and financial receipts when you are elected.

To make fundraising tasks manageable, break details into month-by-month fundraising goals and spending plans. The budget line items that follow provide insight on the potential income and expenditures for your campaign:

Fundraising income comes from cash contributions and in-kind contributions. To guide your fundraising and to keep it visible in your budget, refer to the contributions chart that you built for your campaign plan in Chapter 6.

Campaign expenditure line items vary sensitively as a function of the needs of your particular race, the size of your election district, and the level and strategies of the competition that you face. Each election office has different rules about how to report expenses. Typical expense items include the following:

- Travel, lodging, food, and refreshments
- Broadcast, print, and billboard advertising
- Event expenses for participation in and tickets to shows, fairs, parades
- Production expenses for videos for online distribution and DVD mailers
- Television and radio ad production and spot purchase
- Office rent
- Database and project management

- Website design and hosting

- Design and printing of literature

- Management and consulting service fees

- Postage

- Surveys and polls

- Wages, salaries, and benefits for paid staff

- Wages for paid ballot petition circulators

- Manufacturing costs for campaign marketing items such as yard signs, posters, banners, giveaways, T-shirts, and clothing with campaign logos

Whatever the size of your budget, use it as a tool for recruiting contributors in the months you most need them; for selecting vendors from whom to solicit in-kind contributions; and for making all of your expenditures as cost-effective as possible. The budget can be modified up or down as the campaign plays out. Be sure to keep track of all monies coming in and all monies going out, as well as all in-kind contributions to your campaign. You'll have some level of reporting to do for everything received and spent.

Finally, once you have created your budget, stick to it. If spending needs to increase, make sure you have generated enough contributions to cover the added spending. If you don't raise enough money to cover your spending, determine early what you will have to live without. Be sure to identify the types of expenditures that your campaign will never make.

Building Fundraising Momentum: Endorsements and Money

The day you publically announce your candidacy is the first day of campaign fundraising momentum. Remember from Chapter 5 that most election laws require that you file campaign paperwork with an election office and that you have a treasurer before accepting in-kind or cash contributions. While you may have already collected monies from people you know, now is your official public "ask" for support. You will ask for cash and in-kind support from your campaign team members, from their friends, from civic groups, and from total strangers.

Asking people to endorse you and your candidacy also helps build fundraising momentum. When potential contributors see that people they know are supporting you, they are more likely to support you too. When asking people to endorse you, make sure you have their written permission to publically list them as endorsers or supporters.

Issuing fundraising challenges can also create momentum. For instance, if we raise $5,000 by Friday, we can advertise on the radio for one week. Or, if we raise $10,000 by next Wednesday, we can lock in a billboard placement for the entire month before the election. Or, if we raise $8,000, we can print two thousand yard signs to get the word out about my candidacy. Tying a fundraising challenge to a specific purchase makes your request more tangible and meaningful. People like to know how their money will be spent.

Financial matches can create momentum. During our campaign we had a contributor say that she'd match contributions made during a three-day window, up to a total match of $2,000. It worked. We made an e-announcement to our newsletter subscribers and earned the match!

"Asks" are the acts of requesting funds. They can be made in person, writing, or advertising. Be creative. During 2010, my gubernatorial campaign did a $49.43 "ask" for contributions, because Idaho was the forty-third state admitted to the union and because a contribution under fifty dollars does not require that a contributor's name be submitted to our Secretary of State's Election Office in Idaho. It was a fun and educational "ask" because not everyone remembered that Idaho was state number forty-three. Discover in your community what might serve as a unique, educational, and memorable way to ask for specific dollar amounts. Small amounts add up to big amounts.

Plus, putting to use all of the traditional and online tools for generating contributions keeps your momentum going strong. You'll find more on these tools later in this chapter.

Hard Money, Soft Money, and In-Kind Contributions

Hard money and *soft money* refer to the two basic modes, direct and indirect, by which money can be legally contributed to political campaigns. A third mode of giving is *in-kind contribution*, which is a non-cash input that can be assigned a cash-equivalent value. Not every campaign or candidate receives both hard and soft money. However, it is important for you, your treasurer, and your campaign team to understand hard and soft money because different regulations as to amount, use, and reporting will apply to your campaign, depending on the money's source and use.

Hard money is money contributed directly to your campaign. Remember to check with the election office governing your race for the limits on contributions and for the reporting rules governing each contribution amount. Hard money may be cash, check, online contributions, or in-person credit card amounts. Determine what forms of hard money your campaign will receive. My campaign team preferred checks and online contributions, as well as contributions of services and items.

Soft money is given to political parties, tax-exempt 527 organizations that exist for the purpose of affecting election outcomes, and/or political action committees, any of which then use the money to help build the parties, help candidates in their races, or work against candidates in individual or collective races. As an example, political parties sometimes produce mailers for multiple candidates during an election cycle. Other times political parties will produce a door-to-door piece for multiple candidates and then deliver the piece by using political party volunteers.

In-kind contributions are items or services that you might otherwise purchase but that a contributor is donating free of charge. Here is a sampling of things you might pursue as in-kind contributions to your campaign.

- *Hosting meet-the-candidate or fundraising events*: The food, beverages, invitations, and all event-related expenses may be paid for by the host and recorded by your campaign as an in-kind contribution as long as the amount is under the giving limit.

- *Services*: Volunteers may provide services with monetary value that they'd like to contribute to your campaign. Clerical, database, mailing assembly, and website design services are some examples. Each election district has differing rules about how to record the work of volunteers, and what does and does not have to be recorded in your financial reports. You and your treasurer need to know these rules.

- *Items*: Yard sign stakes, event materials, paper, office supplies, and loans of equipment can help your campaign.

- *Facilities*: A campaign office or phone bank space and system may be offered to you. Again, be sure you know the giving limits.

- *Food and beverage for an event*: Remember to make a determination about your campaign's acceptance and serving of alcohol. Be sure that you have the right campaign insurances in place if you will be serving alcohol.

- *Fees:* entrance fees paid by a contributor or waived by an event holder; fairs, tradeshows, rodeos, and parades all have entrance fees.

Think creatively about what you can ask for in the way of donated services and items. You may be pleasantly surprised at what you get.

■ **Note** Spending the most money doesn't guarantee you'll win. Remember the 2010 race for California governor—the candidate who spent $140 million *less* was the winner.

Tools to Raise Money

Mailings, emails, personal "asks," events, newsletters, letters, and even donation boxes can help you raise money for the campaign. Be sure that your treasurer tracks every source of money, because he or she must have the correct information for reports. What follows are some examples of the tools you may choose to use during your campaign. The bigger your budget, the more you'll need to use every tool listed. The smaller your budget, the more likely you can narrow your list of fundraising tools and still experience fundraising success.

Letters

Letters and envelopes are the most traditional ways to reach out and ask for money. They are followed in importance by fundraising events in people's homes, in restaurants, or in event venues. Letters from the candidate as well as letters from your fundraising chairs are most successful in generating funds. I have seen one candidate use a letter from his mother, though I have no way of knowing how much that campaign earned from that type of "ask."

As an example, I offer the following letter which I sent in 2009 to prior campaign contributors. I wanted to be the first to notify past contributors that I was running for Idaho governor and that I wanted their support, so I was providing them an opportunity to jump in as my first supporters this time around. I printed the letter inside a notecard bearing a four-color image of a watercolor of the Idaho Capitol by a local artist (Figure 8-1).

Candidate Jana M. Kemp
www.VoteKemp.com
Card Art by: Boise Artist Miriam Woito

Paid for by: Jana M. Kemp for House, Myrna M. Benton, Political Treasurer

Figure 8-1. *Notecard.* Artist Miriam Woito painted this image of the Idaho Capitol and granted the author permission to publish it on a notecard, to be used for campaign solicitations, thank-yous, and invitations.

The text of the letter printed inside the notecard depicted in Figure 8-1 was as follows:

> As you may know, I'm running for Governor of Idaho as an Independent in 2010. As a past supporter, you know that it takes a tremendous amount of resources to win an election.

> I'm asking you to join with me today to champion education, entrepreneurial economic development and effective, efficient state services for Idaho.

> Contribute today at www.VoteKemp.com. You may give up to $5,000, the maximum amount allowed by law. Contributions include: cash, in-kind item or service contributions, and hosting events.

> Contact me to share an Idaho concern or an idea you have about how you want to help.

> Thank you! Together, we can make a difference in Idaho's future today!

> Postage Paid For by Vote Jana Kemp, John Smith, Political Treasurer.

Run all of your letters past your messaging team and your fundraising team to be certain that you continue to present a clear and consistent message about why you are running for office. Letters, postcards, and envelopes should also be reviewed by a mail-house or a post office before sending out anything in bulk. You'll want to produce materials that can save you postage as well as generating contributions.

Envelopes

You've probably received a campaign contribution letter that included a pre-addressed form-like envelope to make giving easier. These pre-printed envelopes also help campaign tracking work more smoothly because when filled out completely, these envelopes provide the information that your treasurer needs for reporting and that your volunteer coordinator can use for everything from recruiting volunteers to getting yard signs delivered. Pre-printed campaign envelopes typically include the following elements:

- *Front of the envelope*: This side of the envelope includes your campaign mailing address as the return address in the upper left-hand corner. It shows your campaign address prominently as the mail-to address in the address label block. In the upper right-hand corner where the stamp is placed, you should have this text printed in a small font, which will help you save money: "Your stamp helps. Thanks."

- *Outside of flap*: This portion of the envelope can be printed with information as well. You can show your name, the motto or slogan of the campaign, and your website, along with information about who paid for the envelope production.

- *Inside of flap and back of the envelope*: These areas are typically printed with brief points about your campaign and your request for contributions. This is where you ask people to commit to giving a dollar amount, to hosting an event, to volunteering, or to posting a yard sign. This is also where you want to collect their names, addresses, and method of payment. As a result, you want to lay out a form-like design that allows people to check boxes and write a minimal amount of information. Some envelopes also include spaces for a contributor to list credit card information. Be sure that the printed flap covers the envelope printing and allows for the envelope to be opened without destroying any of the information. An envelope or political product printer can help you with the layout and design.

- *Additional layout design options*: Research has found that leading with a big dollar amount, suggesting dollar amounts, and allowing a contributor to choose a different amount leads to bigger individual contributions, such as:

☐ *I want to make a BIG contribution in small, easy monthly contributions. Please charge my debit/credit card each month until October 20, 2010 in the amount of*
  ☐ *$10* ☐ *$25* ☐ *$50.*

☐ *I want to make a one-time gift of*
  ☐ *$500* ☐ *$250* ☐ *$100* ☐ *$50* ☐ *other amount*

Thank you!!! Together, we can make it happen!

Pre-printed campaign envelopes are a traditional fundraising tool because they help people think about and commit to giving specific things to your campaign. Most often, they are worth the cost of production.

Email

Email "asks," newsletters, and event announcements have been a cost-saving boon to campaigning. Make the most of online communications. Some of my favorite e-fundraisers include challenges such as "Join the $49.43 Club!" matches of contributions where one contributor will match smaller contributions up to a capped dollar amount; and e-house parties. What is an e-house party? Well, the first one I saw was in 2006 from a candidate in Kansas who decided that fundraising could be done via an email "ask" framed as a house party because you get to stay home and contribute online, thereby saving time and travel investments on top of a dollar contribution. The house party invitation read something like this: "We are all busy. So, rather than inviting you to one more event that won't fit into your schedule, we are asking you to learn more about _____ and his campaign for city council. Visit his website _____ to learn more. Use the E-House Party tab at the website to make your contribution. Enjoy the hours you've saved by not attending an event for spending time with your family and friends. Thanks for your support."

Using email to invite people to live events works, too. So does a weekly e-newsletter that includes information about the campaign along with financial contribution requests.

Robocalls

Some candidates like to use automated telephone calls, also known as robo-calls, to ask for contributions. There are services you can hire to perform the production and the delivery of the message. Discover whether these calls work for you or against you in your district. In the last three election cycles, I've been hearing more negatives than positives about their use. However, in your district these recorded message calls may still be working.

Webpage for Your Campaign

With a secure online payment system linked to your campaign website, you can generate significant dollars in contributions without spending any money on postage. Be sure that your webpages include the highlights of your spending plan, and that you appreciate the support. I highly recommend that you use a third-party money handler. You'll pay a handling or administrative fee, but it is worth it. The funds are collected via a secured third-party on behalf of the campaign, the contributor information is securely collected and re-ported, and the money can be directly transferred into your campaign bank account.

Social Media

Social media are a great way to point people to your campaign website, where your secure online payment system will be. Social media are also a vi-able way to invite people to participate in fundraising challenges and events. See Chapter 11 for an extended discussion of the application of social media to online campaigning.

Events

Fundraising events range from house parties and round-ups at a ranch to cocktail parties at country clubs or restaurants, as well as high-ticket seated dinners with auctions and silent auctions. Be sure to check with your election office to learn what is legal on the fundraising front in your state and/or with the Federal Election Committee. Remember that event invitations cost money, the event venue and food costs money, and any special event speakers cost money. Be sure to create event-by-event budgets and track whether contributions at the event not only paid for expenses, but also earned money for the campaign.

More than one candidate has had a political party bigwig come to stump for the campaign only to discover that the costs far outweighed the receipts. For instance, a DC politico coming to stump for you may have travel, secret service, and other expenses associated with the trip that will be billed back to your campaign. Are you ready to foot that bill? If not, say "no, thank you" to the bigwig stumping and stay focused on you, your campaign, and the race you are running.

In-Kind Contribution Forms

Create an in-kind contribution form as a way to prompt giving and to expedite tracking for reporting purposes. We used the following hand-delivered form to solicit in-kind contributions:

IN-KIND CONTRIBUTION

Date _____

JANA KEMP FOR IDAHO GOVERNOR 2010

THE VOICE AND CHOICE FOR INDEPENDENT IDAHO

P.O. Box 8045

Boise, ID 83707

Submitted by: _____

(Name of individual or entity contact person)   please print

Name of company or entity_____

Address: _____

City, State Zip: _____

Phone: _____

Email: _____

Explanation of in-kind donation (room space, refreshments, etc.):

_____

_____

_____

Valuation by donor:_____

(Maximum total contributions limit is $5,000)

Signature of donor or representative: _____

Date:_____

Acceptance:_____ Date:_____

      please print

_____

      Signature

Campaign Treasurer, _____

208.888.8888

email: _____

7/12/09 Kemp In-Kind Form

Donation Boxes

Donation boxes may be deployed at events that your campaign is sponsoring and at which you have designated campaign workers overseeing them. Cash dropped into a donation box without corresponding contributor information causes a recording and reporting dilemma. The donation box attendant must supply the donor a contribution form or contribution envelopes to fill out on the spot.

Which tools work best for fundraising? They all work, yet they have various levels of effectiveness in various races and election districts across the country. To determine what will work best in your district, ask previous candidates, consider hiring a fundraising consultant, and experiment yourself with what works best.

▧ **Note** If you don't ask, you don't raise funds. Be sure to ask for contributions at every opportunity.

Make the Money "Asks"

Just like in sales, you must ask for contributions. This process of asking for financial support is often referred to as making the money "ask." If you don't ask, you won't raise funds. People want to be wanted. They want to hear directly from you why they should support, help, contribute, and vote for you. Even when you ask politely and in person, there will be people whom you've counted as friends and supporters who will not contribute. Keep going. Move on to other individuals and groups and keep asking. As they say in the sales game, it is all about the numbers. The more people you ask, the more contributions you'll get.

Schedule your asking. Whether you make personal phone calls, attend special fundraising events hosted by others, or hold your own fundraising events, you must get fundraising activities onto your campaign calendar. Too many days can pass by without making a single financial "ask." Once out of the asking habit, it is easy to fail to meet your fundraising goals.

Start asking. Keep asking. Ask your team to ask. Expect and ask your fundraising chair to ask. If you don't ask, you won't get the funds you have budgeted to run and win your campaign.

▧ **Note** With money, you have a better chance of winning.

Strategies and Limits

I mentioned earlier our campaign mantra of not spending money unless we had it. Many a candidate has outspent campaign receipts, leaving a debt trail of unpaid vendors. This is not right. Many other candidates have dipped into personal savings and retirement accounts to fund both winning and losing campaigns from which their personal monies are never recouped. Personal loans to a campaign and repayment of the loans are governed by state and federal law and overseen by election offices. Be sure to follow the rules that apply in your election district.

Set your personal contribution limits to the campaign. Stick to them. Know what the legal limits for receiving monies are. Report what must be reported and track everything.

Without money, you are destined to lose. Getting the word out about who you are takes money. As you've discovered, signs, parties, mailings, websites, and parade participation all cost money. Before moving ahead, sit down with your family and agree on the limits of family spending on this campaign. Also, sit down with your treasurer and fundraising chair to agree upon a campaign budget strategy and your spending philosophies. Now is the time to come to agreement on strategy, budgets, and spending so that you don't lose friends and campaign supporters once the race is underway.

Conclusion

Set your fundraising goals and reach them. Without money it is difficult to get the word out about you and your campaign. The more money you raise, the greater your chances of being heard. Remember, if you don't ask, you don't and won't raise funds.

Run: Create Campaign Literature

With your platform, message statements, and budget in hand, you are ready to start producing your campaign literature. Ask your message team to help you craft the statements you'll use on each item that you produce. The variety of campaign literature pieces you produce will depend on the size of your budget and the scope of your race. They may be big enough to warrant producing all of the pieces discussed in this chapter: doorhangers, postcards, letters, posters, bumper stickers, giveaways, T-shirts, and yard signs. Or, your race may be limited enough in budget and scope that you really need only one piece of literature to help you win. Most likely, your race will fall somewhere in between, and you'll pick and choose the most cost-effective pieces for your situation.

Whatever types of literature you decide to produce, design each piece so that it conveys to the voters you are trying to reach exactly who you are and why they should want to vote for you. Then be careful to distribute the literature only in places where people who are likely to consider voting for you will appreciate receiving it. Giving out your literature at an inhospitable venue is a bad investment of your campaign's precious money and time. Indeed, ill-targeted literature can backfire on you, antagonizing people and galvanizing them to vote against you. Passing out Republican literature at an environmental or union rally makes as little sense as passing out Democratic literature at a gun show.

You need people's goodwill so that they will listen to and read about what you have to say. You'll want to be sure that your messages are fine-tuned for a variety of audiences in the event that you can afford to produce a variety of literature pieces. In this chapter you'll learn about the most-often used pieces of campaign literature.

Make Your Point Clearly

The rule in creating any piece of campaign literature: make your point clearly. Start with the message statements, bulleted platforms, and candidate biographies that you've already created (Chapter 7). Then rework and re-purpose these items into a meaningful and complete message that fits the size and function of the piece you are producing.

For example, key points can fit onto a business card. These key points and more can fit onto a candidate information card. Your name or your website—but not both—can fit onto a bumper sticker. The message must be readable under the usual conditions in which most people will see it.

When people can't understand you or your message, they won't vote for you. To make sure your campaign literature is clear and understandable, have your message team and selected supporters review what you plan to print before you have anything printed. You'll be surprised that what you thought was clear might not make sense to others.

Make Your Point Accessible

An accessible message is one that is readable, easy to understand, and easily found. The accessibility of your message statements, platform, and responses to questions will influence whether potential voters will listen or read long enough to decide to vote for you. The more words you use, the more difficult it is for people to follow what you are saying.

In your written information, more text does not equal a better message. People must be able to see and read your message points. This means your pieces must use a large enough font size to be readable, must have the visual interest of photographs and images, and must be presented in a way that is visually and textually interesting.

When writing or speaking, be sure to use language that is professional, not academic. Academic writing and professor-speak will not reach the number of voters you need to win your election. Everyday human-interaction language is the best way to make your messages accessible to the greatest number of people.

Build Name Recognition with Literature

Campaign literature is the most basic need of every candidate's campaign. Without literature, it is nearly impossible to leave a memorable vote-for-me impression in people's hands when they walk away from meeting you, close their door, or get up and leave an event. On all of the following literature pieces, be sure to include your name, the office for which you are running and any legally required paid-for-by information. Beyond that, you can decide what to include. Some candidates list phone numbers, others rely on emails. It's your campaign, so you choose.

Business Cards: The smallest option for a printed message format is a business card. The front and back of a business card can communicate enough information for people to consider voting for you and to point people to your website to learn more (Figure 9-1).

Figure 9-1. *Business card.* The least costly campaign literature piece to produce, the front and back of a business card provides enough information to get voters to remember your name, visit your website, and to remember that they met you in person.

Candidate Information Cards: These cards, both generic and customized to specific audiences, are a must when you can't possibly meet everyone in your election district in person. You use the information cards at events, fairs, talks, debates, and door-to-door introductions. Your campaign team and volunteers use them to introduce you wherever they go too. Information cards provide enough information for people to decide to vote for you. The cards should also point people to your website and social media outlets so that people wanting to do more research on you can get to your official sites. Design your information cards so that printing appears on both sides of the card (Figure 9-2). If you opt to produce a tri-fold piece of literature, be sure the most important information—your name, what you are running for, and that you want the person's vote—are on the front panel. People do not always open up folded literature to read it, so be sure you make an immediate impact on the front panel (Figure 9-3).

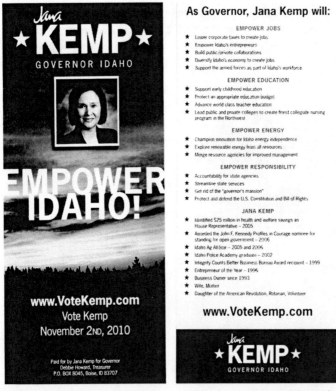

Figure 9-2. *Candidate information card.* This four-color candidate information card was used at trade-shows, fairs, meet-the-candidate events, and as a door-to-door card. If you print only one piece for your campaign, a business card or a candidate information card is a good investment.

Figure 9-3. *Tri-fold candidate literature (front and back).* This example from the author's 2004 campaign served as a mailer and a candidate information card. It identifies the candidate and what she plans to do.

Doorhangers: These are flyers or cards designed to be left at someone's door. Some doorhangers are manufactured with a slit and a hole so that you can literally hang the card on a door knob or door handle. Other doorhangers are plastic bags filled with candidate information and sometimes giveaway items. Some doors do not accommodate hanger-style literature and demand the use of a rubber band. Be prepared for the variety of doors you'll see on the campaign trail.

Doorhangers should provide enough information to let a voter decide to vote for you. Some campaigns print enough candidate information cards to use as doorhangers. Others choose to create a separate piece and use a different design.

Postcard Mailings: These are cost-effective and can range in size from 4 × 6 up to 8 × 10 inches. Check with the post office to be sure your card dimensions are correct to qualify for the best bulk-mail postage rates. Many printers can produce beautiful four-color postcards fairly cheaply. Some candidates choose to use postcard mailings to reach out to registered voters. Others choose to send postcards to every address in their district, hoping to pick up some new voters. If your funds are limited, choose just the registered-voter list. Postcard mailings can be sent once or in sequence over weeks and months. Bear in mind the rule of thumb in advertising: the average person needs to see your name at least seven times before she'll remember you. Postcards can be used to share information about who you are and to invite voters to meet-the-candidate events.

Postcard mailings can be as inexpensive as one-color ink on colored paper (Figure 9-4). Postcards can also be elaborate four-color productions, which work best for photographs (Figure 9-5). Postcard production can be driven by your campaign or by a party ally's campaign. Your campaign may or may not be asked to chip in to pay for the piece. Be sure in either event to find out what election rules apply. For an example, see Figure 9-6, which was produced by a then-congressman and specific to the election district in which I and two others were running.

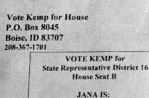

Figure 9-4. *One-color postcard (front and back).* When budgets are tight, one-color mailings to targeted voters can be effective communication pieces.

Figure 9-5. *Four-color postcard mailer (back and front).* This 2006 reminder-to-vote card communicated that the candidate had served well and requested that she be re-elected.

Figure 9-6. *Co-op postcard mailer (front and back).* This 2004 postcard was produced by the congressman running for the U.S. House. His team produced this mailer to present four candidates to voters in Idaho District 16.

Letter Mailings: Letters are a great way to reach out personally to voters, and to ask for money. Well-funded campaigns use both letters and postcards. Most of us have budgets that require us to choose one or the other. Form letters with names dropped in by a printer can be used to reach people you don't know. Personalized letters can be sent to people who know you. Thank-you letters should be sent to everyone who contributes time and/or money to your campaign.

Fundraising Letter Mailings: Covered in Chapter 8, these mailings are your tools for generating cash and in-kind contributions. You can sign them, or the letters can come from your fundraising chair or other campaign supporters who are well-known in your community (Figure 9-7).

Candidate Jana M. Kemp
www.VoteKemp.com
Card Art by: Boise Artist Miriam Woito

If you want a governor who will -
★ Relieve Idaho of the "Governor's Mansion." No one lives in it and it costs taxpayers thousands of dollars annually.
★ Appoint and hire women and men based on their skills and expertise for the job of serving Idaho.
★ Audit all departments for improvements (in 2005/2006 I recommended $25M in savings for the Department of Health and Welfare).
★ Work with all colleges and universities to prepare 21st Century Teachers to serve 21st Century Kids.
★ Create early childhood learning opportunities that don't now exist.

★ Establish Scholarships for two-year, four-year and advanced degree students who will serve businesses in Idaho.
★ Establish Medical Savings Accounts that NEVER go away (if the money isn't used, you get to KEEP it – it is YOUR money after all!). And,
★ *Really* grow existing businesses in and recruit new businesses to Idaho.

Support Jana Kemp, Independent Candidate for Governor 2010.
Donate online: www.VoteKemp.com
Donate by mail: Jana Kemp for Governor,
PO Box 8045, Boise, ID 83707

Paid for by Vote Jana Kemp, Governor 2010
Political Treasurer: Debbie Howard

Thank You! You'll love the results!!

Figure 9-7. *Fundraising mailer.* Notecards from an earlier campaign were repurposed by having the printer cut off the line with the former political treasurer's information and print on the card interior the 2010 request for financial contributions, along with the current treasurer's information. Blank cards can sometimes be printed on office printers; other times a print shop is your best bet. This fundraising mailer on the Jana Kemp signature notecard always got noticed and generated responses that both paid for the mailing and raised monies.

Posters: If you have the funds and the locations to post them, posters are an eye-catching way to get people to notice you and your candidacy. Plus, a poster in a location means the facility has given you permission, which usually means at least one person at the site plans to vote for you. Creative designs that reinforce your name, your campaign, what you believe in, and your website work the best.

Bumper Stickers: Advertise your name and website at high velocity or in a traffic jam. Make sure what you produce is readable at driving speeds and distances. Tip: be sure to specify to your printer whether or not you want a union symbol on the finished product. Most bumper stickers are produced at union shops. Bumper stickers work effectively when applied to bumpers, vehicle windows, posters, yard signs, and things you carry, such as clipboards (Figure 9-8).

Figure 9-8. *Bumper sticker.* Bumper stickers are cost-effective ways to get the word out and moving around town. Plus, bumper stickers can be applied to objects that are in use by the campaign to build even more name recognition, such as the clipboard shown here.

Giveaways: Buttons, stickers, pencils, pens, balloons, candy, refrigerator magnets, and a variety of other campaign knick-knacks fit into this category. These items are used to build name recognition with the recipients and with the people who see the recipients sporting them. Check your state laws about what you can give away. Some states' laws are so strict that you may not give away anything but printed paper literature.

T-Shirts and Clothing: These items are considered here because they serve as media for text and they fit into your menu of alternatives for allocating your literature budget. T-shirts, hats, or jackets emblazoned with your name and message can reinforce who you are, the race you are in, and where people can go to learn more about you and your candidacy. Plus, volunteers and supporters like wearing regulation issue that identifies them as soldiers in your campaign. See Figure 9-9 for some examples.

Figure 9-9. *T-shirts.* Campaign clothing can range from inexpensive T-shirts, as shown here, to expensive shirts, jackets, and vests. Volunteers like to have campaign clothing to wear.

Websites and Social Media: See Chapter 11. Bottom line: get online! Visit www.JanaKemp.com/VoteKemp for an example of a full-blown campaign website. This example shows how the campaign site looked from the day of the election.

Yard Signs: When done right, yard signs (such as Figure 9-10) are cost-effective, creative, and colorful, and they do their job of building name recognition. Be sure that they are readable. In other words, don't make the graphics too complex and the number of words too many. Simple is better. Be sure to include the proper paid-for-by information on the signs. Yard signs must be weather-durable. The yard sign stakes that are most easy to install are the H-stake design. Some people use rebar, but this is usually more difficult to install and remove. Be sure to assign volunteer sign- placement teams to place signs beginning one month before Election Day. Also appoint and monitor sign pick-up teams to clean up the night of and days after the election.

Figure 9-10. *Yard sign.* Produce easy-to-read yard signs to get your name out in drive-by locations. The goal with yard signs is name recognition.

Billboards: Free-standing banners and digital billboards are additional possibilities for reaching out to voters—as are mobile billboards on buses, trucks, and personal or for-hire passenger vehicles. Billboard purchases must typically be made three months to a year or more before you want the billboard to go up, which is limited to the last month before the election in most cases.

Figure 9-11. *License plate.* Customized license plates turn your vehicle into a moving campaign sign. This plate started many conversations about who was in the race for governor.

Figure 9-13. *Event signage.* This poster-style sign was a good promotional tool at booths and speaking engagements. The three-foot-square size and stiff backing made it a bit difficult to transport.

Figure 9-12. *Roll-up banner.* This three-feet-wide by eight-feet-tall portable, light-weight banner rolls into its base for easy packing and carrying. It was well received for four years of events, tradeshow and fair booths, and speaking opportunities. Banners with your picture always draw attention.

Unique Message Vehicles: For starters, your car can serve as a moving bill-board. You can be as bold as having vinyl lettering put on your vehicle win-dows, which I did, and included my name, what I was running for, and the campaign website. Or, you can be as subtle as purchasing a customized li-cense plate, which I also did (Figure 9-11). Traditional and specialty banners are also worthwhile investments if you'll be working any event circuits. See Figure 9-12, which shows a 3 × 8 foot roll-up banner that served two of my three races well, because it has my picture, my name, and the campaign website. For tradeshows, simple signage works best (Figure 9-13). Our campaign even had a self-propelled campaign float that appeared in a dozen pa-rades and in a car show as recently as the spring of 2011. Remember, alert the media to cover your appearances as much as you can (Figure 9-14).

Figure 9-14. *Magazine cover.* Keep yourself in the news. Name recognition happens when you are visible in person and in print.

You can print items on your home computer or use a professional printer. Whatever you choose to do, be sure that your materials look professional enough to invite people to read about you and to vote for you. Just as you would for a business, get bids, and be sure that you have a clear agreement about what finished products will look like and what they will cost.

For full-color images of all the campaign pieces depicted and discussed in this chapter, please visit www.JanaKemp.com/RunForOffice.

Control Your Campaign Message

Print what you want distributed. Having others create material for you tends to create a loss of control about what you are really saying. Review what you put into print. Where possible, review what others put into print about you.

You are the candidate. You are the one with the message. Others can help you distribute the message, but you must remain in control of your messages and outreach so that potential voters learn the truth about you and what you want to do.

Keep control of your campaign and its messages. It is your campaign and your responsibility to deliver information from which people can decide to vote for you.

Get Endorsements

Endorsements come in several forms. They are often testimonials by individuals about what a great candidate you are, together with their names. Endorsements are also lists of names of people who support you and your candidacy. Finally, endorsements can come from a group, a political action committee, or an elected official. The use of endorsements can help you reach people whom you may never meet in person. When people see names they recognize and admire on a list or in a quoted endorsement, they are more likely to pay attention to what you have to say.

Endorsements for fundraising purposes were touched on in Chapter 8. Endorsements help persuade people to contribute to your campaign and to vote for you. When someone has never met you, yet recognizes the name of someone he or she does know, you have a better chance of getting noticed and earning another vote.

Sometimes candidate surveys are solely for the purpose of providing information to a group's membership. Other times candidate surveys are used to identify and select candidates that a group wants to endorse to its members and to the public. In some cases, group endorsements are accompanied by campaign contributions of cash and/or legwork such as flyer delivery and yard sign postings. Pursue the groups that you'd like to endorse you, and ask for details about what their endorsement includes and/or requires from you in return.

Endorsement lists and quotes can be used in a variety of places. Traditional spots include newspaper advertisements and campaign letterhead. More and more, endorsements are featured on campaign websites and social media platforms. Be sure that you have documented permission from individuals to use their endorsements in your campaign. Use the endorsements in several ways so that you can reach more voters: advertisements; campaign flyers; letter or postcard mailings.

Sample Candidate Card Content

If you only produce one giveaway piece of literature, produce a candidate information card or flyer. Depending on how you flexibly you design the piece, you and your volunteers can distribute it everywhere: door-to-door; event speaking; public appearances; hand-shaking; and in envelope and postcard mailings.

When designing the card, be sure your message is clear and readable. Also, be sure to include your platform, key points, and campaign slogan (my 2010 slogan was "Empower Idaho!"), so that your message is consistent in print and online. You'll want a card that is eye-catching and prompts people to read the information. Include your campaign website on the card so people can learn more about you if they choose to do more research. Obviously, your name and the office for which you are running also need to be on the card.

People's time and attention are short so the best candidate cards are two-sided and can fit into a number ten envelope. On the front of the card, place your name, the office for which you are running, your website, and the paid-for-by information required by election laws. Also include the party with which you are running, if the election is partisan and you are not running as an independent. There are a variety of theories about the advantages and disadvantages of declaring the candidate's party on the candidate card. My policy is be honest and tell prospective voters whether I'm affiliated with a party, running as an independent, or running for a non-partisan position. Use a photograph that is eye-catching. If people only look at this side, you want to provide enough information to earn a vote.

On the back of the card, include your platform key points and some of your biographical information. You want to communicate who you are and what your campaign is about. Use clear, readable, short message points. People who turn the card over are looking for more information about you so they can decide whether to vote for you. Incorporate photos and images that help to tell the story without making the design too crowded or too difficult to read. Direct people to your website to learn more about you and your positions. The copy on the back of my 2010 candidate information card (Figure 9-2) follows:

JANA KEMP - BIOGRAPHICAL INFORMATION

- Identified $25 million in Health & Welfare Savings as House Representative in 2005

- John F. Kennedy Profiles in Courage Nominee in 2006 for standing for Open Government

- Idaho Ag All Star 2005 & 2006

- Idaho Police Academy Graduate 2002

- Integrity Counts Better Business Bureau Award Recipient 1999

- Entrepreneur of the Year 1996

As governor, Jana Kemp will:

Empower Jobs – Champion Job Creation:

- Diversify Idaho's economy

- Empower entrepreneurs

- Grow private and non-profit jobs

- Build public/private/non-profit collaborations

- Lower corporate taxes to create jobs

- Ensure national recognition of Idaho's military contributions

Empower Education – Leader for our Future and Economy:

- Support early childhood education

- Protect an appropriate education budget

- Advance world-class teacher education

- Lead public & private colleges to create the finest collegiate nursing program in the northwest

Empower Energy & Resources – Champion Innovation:

- Pursue Idaho energy independence
- Explore renewable energy from all resources
- Merge resource agencies for improved management
- Merge water and energy agencies for improved planning and management

Empower Responsibility – Model Walking the Talk:

- Accountability for state agencies
- Streamline state services
- Return the "governor's mansion" to the donors
- Open government through weekly updates from the Governor's office
- Expect non-profits to meet more community needs
- Build a culture of open government and protected First Amendment rights—we have the brain-power to solve our problems and to innovate!
- Protect and defend the U.S. Constitution and Bill of Rights

For more information, please visit: www.VoteKemp.com

For additional full-color examples of the campaign pieces discussed here, please visit www.JanaKemp.com/RunForOffice.

Note Tell people who you are and what you are about. Not everyone will choose to vote for you—that's okay. Keep telling the story of who you are and what you will do in office, so that people can choose to vote for you.

No Campaign Literature? Plan to Lose Your Race

People must know who you are, why you are running, and what you plan to do once elected. When voters do not know these key points about you, they tend to vote for the political party of a candidate or for the most-recognized name.

Continue to refine your message so that you can tell your story and get yourself elected. Literature tells your story when you are not present to tell the story yourself. Literature helps others tell the story when you are not available in person to answer questions. Literature is a commitment in writing that communicates who you are and what you will do in office.

Conclusion

Create and distribute campaign materials that tell your story in a way to get you noticed the first time, and again and again. Your literature should build your name recognition so people will remember it when the time comes to vote for YOU.

Run: Employ Traditional Campaign Media

With your message statements clear and your candidate information card or flyer in hand, you can draw from these well-crafted words to be sure your messages are consistent across all media. Traditional campaign media include direct mail, print and broadcast media, billboards, and yard signs. Depending on the size, location, and competitiveness of your election district you may choose to use one, two, or all of the following traditional campaign outreach methods:

Direct Mail: Letters and Postcards: We've all received one or more direct mail pieces from a candidate. Start collecting and studying the ones you receive so that you can note what features you will incorporate in your mailings. These letters, cards, and postcards are part of the name recognition-building aspect of your campaign, as well as part of your fundraising outreach (see Chapter 8). Over the last century, general direct mail has ranged in effectiveness between a one-percent and ten-percent response rate. Over the last two decades, response rates have dropped to three percent or less. So, make sure your direct-mail budget is wisely spent. As much as possible, target your mailing lists to people who are registered to vote, especially those who plan to vote with an absentee ballot. Reach out to party members when you can secure these voter lists from the party with which you have affiliated. Also, be sure to ask the mail-house who handles your mailing to perform a merge/purge of duplicate names and addresses as well as a National Change of Address database check to eliminate addresses at which people are no longer living.

Press Conferences: You can call a press conference on your own. The political party with which you are affiliated may hold press conferences, so let them know you want to participate. Press conferences are announced via press releases, which are discussed elsewhere in this chapter. Press conferences can be held to announce your candidacy, announce a major campaign challenge or platform that is newsworthy, or to respond to a current issue that has arisen in your community and election district. Invite supporters to attend the press conference so that the media in attendance believe that people other than you care about the issue. Also be aware that in these days of traditional media retrenchment, most media organizations are so short-staffed that getting a reporter to your press conference is far from automatic. Regardless, send your press releases to radio stations, print media, political and community bloggers, and television stations.

Town Hall Meetings: Whether in person or via telephone calls, town hall meetings can create media buzz and an in-print news story. The town hall meetings must focus on timely, relevant, hot-button topics. Invite the general public, your voting base, and the media.

Radio: Ads, Interviews, and Candidate Forums: Radio ads can provide cost-effective outreach in districts where people actively and regularly listen to the radio. Ask for demographics from stations so you can be sure that you are reaching the right potential voters. Interviews and candidate forums are free.

Television: Ads, Interviews, and Debates: When considering television advertising, determine whether you have the budget. This is the most expensive form of campaign advertising. Television ads require filming, editing, and the purchase of time on channels that will reach your potential voters. Be aware that you may be paying to reach more people than you need to, depending on the size of your election district. On the other hand, television interviews and debates cost you only your preparation and participation time. Some stations host or broadcast candidate debates. Just because you are a candidate doesn't mean the debate hosts and/or stations will invite you to participate; they neglected to contact me in my independent candidacy of 2010. This means that you and your team must keep a constant watch on organizations and television stations planning to hold debates. Become qualified to participate in as many debates and forums as possible, especially if they are going to be televised.

Newspaper Ads: Placements in daily, weekly, and monthly newspapers should all be considered. Additionally, newspaper-style publications targeting special-interest and trade groups and trade will often take advertisements. Seniors are active voters, so an ad in a publication targeting them often makes sense. Ask for details on the circulation of the newspapers you are considering. Sometimes a newspaper covers more people than you need to reach, which means you are paying for outreach that does you no good. Determine whether you can pinpoint zipcode-specific delivery to make the most of your campaign advertising dollars. We found that monthly special-interest publications, such as senior newspapers, were the best investment because of their target audience, cost-effectiveness, and multiple readers per copy.

Magazine Ads: Magazines are produced with a variety of focal points and in a variety of formats: community, state-wide, newspaper inserts, city-specific, special-interest groups, and trade publications. The cost of advertising in a magazine can range from very reasonable to very expensive. When you consider whether to purchase a magazine ad, be sure to determine whether the publication even reaches the voters you need to reach. Age-specific, family-focused, and region-specific and special-interest publications will be your best investments. All ads must include the paid-for-by information. On rare occasions a magazine may feature you in a story.

Billboards and Posters: Freestanding and public transit billboards can be useful in rural and inner-city districts. Posters are great for places your targeted voters meet, hang-out, or go to shop. They work on your behalf twenty-four hours a day and always deliver the same message about who you are, what you are running for, and where to get more information (your website). Billboards are most effective when:

- Your name is large enough to be read as people drive by
- The office for which you are running is on the sign
- Your website is on the sign

Don't forget; all signs must include the paid-for-by information as required by election law.

Yard Signs: Signs placed in residential and commercial yards and easements tell people you are in the race. This is the most cost-effective way ($4 to $10 apiece) to get your name out all over town. Yard signs are visible for the month before the election. Yard signs also serve as an endorsement because whoever puts a sign in his or her yard is telling the neighborhood they plan to vote for you. Be vigilant that yard signs, once put up, stay up. Sign-stealing and sign-placement wars happen in every campaign to varying degrees. Don't sweat it—just keep getting your signs into yards where they stay posted. Yard signs are also most effective when

- Your name is large enough to be read as people drive by

- The office for which you are running is on the sign

- Don't forget: all signs must include the paid-for-by information as required by election law!

Whatever the traditional media where you buy ads or seek free coverage, keep your message consistent, clear, and accessible.

Tried and Not Always True

Television is a tried, but no longer always true, traditional campaign medium. Fractured viewing among network, cable, and internet lineups; the shrinking presence of televisions in households headed by tech-savvy voters; and the growth in commercial-free viewing by means of such devices as DVR recorders: all these trends make television an increasingly questionable use of often limited campaign funds. Deciding to use television means that you have done the homework and can prove that television advertising will reach the voters you need to convince to vote for you.

Newspaper advertising is another tried, but no longer always true, traditional campaign medium. The same rules apply as in television. Your campaign team must know who is being reached by the ads and whether the ads will reach the voters you need to reach. With online news on the rise, both television viewing and newspaper subscriptions are down. Placing online ads is a different advertising purchase than buying directly from a television station or a newspaper (see Chapter 11).

Be sure that you and your team have researched which traditional media will reach the voters you need to reach and are most cost-effective for your campaign.

The Science of Campaigning

This book is a crash course on getting ready to run a campaign for any office at any level of community involvement or government. Other sources get into the nitty-gritty of campaign messaging, mud-slinging, self-preservation, use of campaign funds, and posturing for the gamesmanship of politics. This book is focused on truthful campaigns that restore dignity and respect to the process of campaigning and serving in elected office. To that end, here is an ultra-short crash course on the science of campaigning:

- *Build Your Name Recognition*: People must know who you are and what seat you are running for before they can vote for you.

- *Communicate Who You Are*: Share why you are capable to do the job and what you value. Value statements should be on nearly every direct-mail piece.

- *Share What You'll Do*: Express what you intend to do once you are on the job. People want to know who you are and what issues you will address before they decide to vote for you.

- *Keep Building Name Recognition*: People must both know and remember who you are and what seat you are running for so they will remember to vote for you.

- *Be Seen in Person, on Television, and in Print*: People need to know that you are a real person whom they can relate to, and for whom they can ultimately cast their ballots.

Campaigning is a numbers game: pursuing the number of votes you need to win. Voters must know you exist before they can vote for you. Get the word out and keep getting the word out that you are in the race and that you are their best choice.

How to Talk to Reporters

Build a relationship with the television, print, and radio reporters in your community and election district. Be seen as a worthwhile person to quote. Offer insights and quotable sayings or sentences. Building a relationship can be as simple as introducing yourself in person and as time-consuming as sending weekly press releases to all reporters.

Stand tall, be proud, but not overly-confident, convey care, and give short, quotable responses. Be intelligent. Stay on your message. Don't let reporters put words in your mouth—they will try to do this anyway, so be prepared and don't get trapped.

Reporters want to talk with and interview people who make sense, who can deliver short and meaningful responses, and who present themselves professionally on camera. Reporters want stories that will capture the interest of readers and listeners.

Create Press Releases

Press releases are well-written statements from you and your campaign sent to people in all media outlets that cover the election district in which you are running. You need to produce press releases, because news organizations are so short-staffed that they rely on getting information from candidates in order to determine what stories to tell. Press releases may land you interviews that result in quotes in print or on broadcasts. Press releases may generate a conversation in the community. Press releases can always be posted on your campaign website to show that you are reaching out to media and the community to share your campaign story. Press releases can be shortened to key message points and posted on social media sites as well.

In studying these three examples, remember that you want to issue press releases on subjects about which you are passionate and can interview well, whether on radio or television or with print reporters. The point is that every press release should evoke a strong emotion, so that you will be more likely to get news media coverage. You want to motivate readers of your press release to pick up the phone to get an in-person airable or printable interview.

But remember—always provide enough information in a press release that an article can be written without your necessarily getting a phone call. Even when the media doesn't show up to a press conference, or comment on your press release in their medium, you can share online what you want people to know.

Different occasions call for differently constructed press releases. Three examples of press releases from my 2010 campaign follow:

Example A. My candidacy announcement, closely drawn on my message statements and platform.

Example B. My critique of a political scandal.

Example C. My policy statement relevant to a high-profile news story.

Example A: A Candidacy Announcement

Voters now have a real choice: Jana Kemp announces candidacy for Idaho governor today; seeks to attract the majority of voters who've lost faith in both parties

Kemp pledges to bring experience in business and government to job

January 5, 2010

For more information, contact:

Jana Kemp – Candidate for Governor: 208-367-1701

www.facebook.com/kemp2010

www.twitter.com/janakemp

www.votekemp.com

Jana Kemp, a businesswoman and former state legislator, announced her candidacy for governor Tuesday, January 5, on a platform of jobs, education, energy, fairness, and responsibility.

"In my business and my public life, my passion is to help organizations succeed by establishing clear goals, empowering the people who do the work, and replacing failed leadership," said Kemp, speaking to a crowd of supporters and the media at the Nampa Civic Center. "In Idaho, we have the intelligence, the creativity and the work ethic to overcome our temporary
challenges. I want to empower all of us to use our gifts, apply them where they will do the most good, and contribute to the bright and exciting future of Idaho."

Kemp, 44, moved from Minnesota to Idaho in 1994 and has a lengthy resume as a business owner, author, speaker, and volunteer; see her website and Facebook page for details.

Kemp is an independent candidate and not affiliated with any political party. She was a Republican state legislator from 2004–2006 representing Northwest Boise. But, paraphrasing Ronald Reagan when he shifted his alignment from the Democratic Party in 1962, Kemp says of her experience: "I didn't leave the party; the party left me."

Kemp says neither party is able to represent Americans well, a point that most Americans already know. According to a September 2009 Rasmussen poll, sixty percent believe neither Republican nor Democratic political leaders have an understanding of what is needed today. More than seventy percent of Republicans and unaffiliated voters say the neither party has the answers. Democrats are more evenly divided.

"This is the perfect time for an independent to run for governor in Idaho, and the need has never been greater," Kemp said. "We know the popularity of the Democratic Party isn't high in Idaho and the infighting in the Republican Party has created a lack of leadership. Many pro-business, pro-entrepreneurial and very religious people feel the Republican Party has left them."

Kemp said there is a strong likelihood the national sentiment toward getting rid of incumbents from either party will lend itself, in Idaho, to people not voting for either party.

Kemp also said the nuts and bolts of good governance are best kept free from partisan influences, and she has outlined a five-point platform regarding jobs, education, energy, fairness and responsibility.

- Economic policy: lower corporate taxes and create a business-friendly environment; mend relations with the state's high-tech and creative sectors; and promote home-grown small business, as well as increase efforts to attract businesses from out of state.

- Education: Increase number of Idahoans enrolling in college (Idaho ranks in the bottom ten states in percent of college graduates in the population); promote early childhood education; protect the education budget from being raided for transportation and other programs.

- Energy: All-of-the-above strategy, including promoting conservation and efficiency, and renewable, nuclear, and low-carbon fossil energy.

- Fairness: Give Idaho homeowners a seven-year rolling average valuation for property tax assessment, to ensure taxes don't go up when housing values go down; resist federal programs that tell Idahoans what to do, how to live, and where to spend our money; and respect legislators and members of the public even if they disagree with her and oppose her.

- Responsibility: Government must live within its means; listen to citizens and learn from what they have to say; have transparency, so citizens can see who is influencing government, and why.

Jana Kemp is the first person to be qualified (the Secretary of State certifies candidates in March 2010) to be on the November 2, 2010 general election ballot for governor. Kemp also invited people today to join the $49.43 club in support of her campaign. Visit www.VoteKemp.com to contribute and get involved.

Paid for by: Jana Kemp for Governor; John Smith, Political Treasurer

Example B: A Political Scandal Critique

From the Jana Kemp Campaign

Independent Candidate for Governor of Idaho

REMARKS

**REMARKS CONCERNING THE SALE OF
IDAHO'S GOVERNOR'S MANSION**

FOR MORE INFORMATION CONTACT:

NAME of your Contact and PHONE NUMBER

www.VoteKemp.com

October 4, 2010

Jana Kemp, Independent Candidate for Governor

I'm Jana Kemp, the independent candidate for Idaho governor.

In November of 2005, the Simplot family donated a house for use as a governor's mansion.

It was a sweet deal for the Simplot family. The state of Idaho would own the house and about one-half of the land surrounding the house—but NOT the road, NOT the walls, NOT the irrigation system, NOT the stables, NOT the ponds, NOT the whole "hill the people ice-block down."

Idaho taxpayers pay for the maintenance of both house and land. That maintenance costs Idaho taxpayers over one hundred thousand dollars every year.

Governor Otter never has and never will live in the mansion. It cannot be used by any governor without extensive and costly modifications.

Idahoans are paying for a house that sits EMPTY.

This is an unnecessary and extravagant expense. It's time to get rid of this hilltop monument to government waste.

The second reason to get rid of the empty house is that the State of Idaho is NOT living up to the laws that the rest of us as business owners would have to if we wanted to lease the property as an event center.

When I am governor, we will dispose of this empty house the way many of us get rid of white elephants and useless possessions.

We'll put the governor's mansion on eBay.

We will offer the governor's mansion to buyers all over the world. We'll sell it to the highest bidder, who may end up being the Simplots after all. We will save the state hundreds of thousands of dollars during my first term in office with that one act.

I'm Jana Kemp. I'm running for governor. If you think this is a good idea, I have plenty more.

Example C: A Policy Statement Relevant to a News Story

VOTE KEMP Press Release *(Spring 2010)*

For more information, contact: Jana Kemp, 208-367-1701

"The death of Robert Manwill has revealed some challenges facing our child welfare system in Idaho," says Idaho gubernatorial candidate Jana Kemp, who is calling for a comprehensive review of children under state supervision to determine how many of them are in homes where an adult has been convicted of seriously injuring a child.

"I want to first say that the people who work in the Idaho Department of Health and Welfare are doing the best job they can in a system that doesn't make child safety enough of a priority," said Kemp. "The system appears to have some inherent faults and in the months following Robert Manwill's death, we have also seen that the leadership and vision to address these faults doesn't currently exist in the governor's office—which can tell us how many wolves live in Idaho, but not how many children live in a home where an adult has been convicted of seriously injuring a child."

Kemp said citizens need answers to these and other questions: How many Idaho children are in the care of people who have been convicted of seriously injuring children? Are there any people caring for children under the supervision of Health and Welfare who are using illegal drugs? Why do we even allow people convicted of seriously injuring children to care for children?

To improve child safety in Idaho, Kemp proposes the following:

- A top-to-bottom assessment of child protection services in Health and Welfare. At minimum, we need to know how many other children are in homes where there is a record of children being seriously injured.

- No adult convicted in court of intentionally, criminally and seriously injuring a child (burning, breaking bones, concussions, choking, sexual abuse, dangerously filthy living environment, exposure to meth labs, etc.) should be allowed to retain custody or care for a child. In the Manwill case, his mother was convicted of fracturing the skull of her infant daughter, yet was still allowed to care for her daughter.

- As a further precaution, anyone under the supervision of Health and Welfare who has responsibility for caring for children should be subject to random drug and alcohol testing. While there is no public knowledge of drug or alcohol involvement in the Manwill case, Kemp supports this as another common-sense precaution, and last week took a drug test herself to set an example of her ability to walk-the-talk of being responsible and living up to the standards to which she speaks of upholding. If parents under Department of Health and Welfare supervision are found to be abusing substances, they must, at minimum, submit to counseling, and pass another test within two weeks or lose custody of their children.

"Adults come under the supervision of Health and Welfare because the children in their care were in crisis, in dangerous situations, or the adults are foster parents," Kemp said. "In either case, we adults must be able to provide safe and healthy care for children or not be allowed to care for children."

Kemp said the current system gives equal weight to parental rights as it does child safety. She said the orientation needs to be shifted so that child safety is paramount. Also, she said the changes don't apply to spanking, but to people who have been convicted of seriously injuring children.

"I do not believe this is a huge population of people, but we need to have an assessment to even know for sure," Kemp said. "The goal here is not to break up families or intrude on parental rights. It is only about removing children from homes where an adult has been convicted of seriously injuring a child. The physical safety of children should be the baseline for the state's decision making."

#END#

Getting Coverage

There are a few ways to ensure you get media coverage, but most of them are the wrong kind of media coverage. For instance, getting arrested, being in an accident, or saying something so ridiculous that you land in the news. Recall these examples of the ridiculous: Rick Perry's 2011 dating of the American Revolution to the 16th century; Sarah Palin's 2011 version of Paul Revere's mission; and of course Howard Dean's 2004 scream.

What you and your campaign want and need are positive stories in the news about you, why you are a worthy candidate, and why people should vote for you. Schedule yourself into events where large crowds gather and the media covers the happenings. Participate in forums and debates that will be covered in the news. Accept radio show invitations. Explore what is happening in your election district that is likely to be covered by the media.

The Twenty-First Century Media Reality

Despite the fracturing of television viewership and newspaper readership, there are still voters to be reached through these mediums. Despite the short-staffing in all news media, every outlet is hungry for well-told and interesting stories.

As a candidate, offer your best information and platform statements as stories. Remember that news outlets are looking for controversial stories. They are also watchful of where their advertising dollars come from and are more likely to cover stories from candidates who have money. It is a fact that has been borne out for over a century. In the 2010 election, I witnessed several races not being fully covered by the media. Print and broadcast media covered selected candidates rather than all the candidates in each race.

My team saw this happen in Congressional races and state legislative and executive branch races. My opinion: news and journalistic media that fail to mention in every article related to an election the names of all of the candidates in that race are guilty of partiality and prejudice wholly at odds with their professional and civic responsibilities as objective reporters. So, you and your team have to work extra hard to get you and your candidacy equally covered in the news.

Prepare Yourself and Your Message for Media

Make sure you are well rested. If you feel tired, you'll look tired in photographs and on television. Look and dress your campaign best at all times because you never know when a camera or a reporter will show up. Practice your message and platform statements so that they are short, clear, repeatable, and polished, but not boring! Practice in front of supporters so they can give you honest and constructive feedback. Practice your speeches while driving. Watch yourself in the mirror to be sure you are using expressions that people can relate to and trust. Your written and spoken messages must be consistent, so stay on point and keep your responses to questions short. Traditional media all require short, quotable messages.

Note Traditional media require short, quotable messages.

No Media Plan? What Now?

It bears repeating: people must know who you are, why you are running, and what you plan to do once elected. When voters do not know these key points about you, they tend to vote for the political party of a candidate or for the most recognized name. Control your message so that you can tell your story and get yourself elected. Produce traditional media pieces and get coverage in traditional media outlets so that you can continually tell your story to voters and earn votes.

Conclusion

Create a traditional media plan and support it with your online and social media efforts (see next chapter) so that you reach voters of all ages, from all backgrounds, and all across your voting district. It is impossible to meet every voter in your district. So, your use of traditional media is key to reaching the voters with whom you'll never have face-to-face time. It also serves to reinforce your effect on voters with whom you have already had face-to-face time.

Run: Employ Online and Social Media

In the first decade of the twenty-first century, online and social media tools became permanent forces affecting the outcomes of elections at all levels. In the 2008 presidential election, President Obama proved this, even hiring campaign staff that included a team dedicated to social media. Yes, your campaign must have an online presence, even if it is just a homepage for your website.

If you want to attract voters thirty-five and younger to your campaign to vote for you with any great impact, you must have an online and social media strategy to reach them. Campaigns, churches, and businesses are all exploring their online and social media strategies to be sure that they are reaching young constituents, congregation members, and customers. Depending on your age and occupation, taking your campaign online will be as natural as breathing, or as daunting as deep sea diving. Whatever your outlook, online methods of communication and outreach are here to stay. So get your campaign online.

Create a Website

The minimum online presence you must have is a campaign website. Look up the candidates you are running against, and also candidates whom you admire in other races, to see what they posted on their campaign websites. Also study the incumbent's websites, both his official government webpage and his standalone political website.

The beauty of online tools is that you can find hundreds of items in a matter of moments. In fact, take time to type your name in a search and see what is already online about you. Some of this information may help you build your website. Some of the information you find may need to be countered or corrected on your official campaign website.

The key elements of a campaign website are the following:

- *Candidate Homepage*: Every candidate handles this differently. What you include on the homepage should be enough information that a voter could decide to vote for you, even without looking at another page.

- *Your Platform*: Post the key points and support them with details. The key points should mirror what you have published on your candidate cards and flyers. The website is really the only place someone can find details about you and what you believe in. So, support your campaign messages on your site.

- *Biographical Information*: People want to know who you are so they can figure out whether they relate to you and like you. Just like they did in high school, people vote for people they like. So, share where you were born, where you grew up, and where you live. Tell people why you care enough to run for office. Share something about your current family, how many kids and grandkids you have. Disclose what you and your spouse currently do to make a financial living.

- *Contribute*: Some people will mail you checks. Others will prefer the convenience and immediacy of contributing online. So provide a secured method of making an online contribution to your campaign. As recommended in Chapter 8, select a third-party vendor that can ensure the safety of collected information and record the transactions for reporting purposes.

- *Get Involved*: Your website is a great place to recruit volunteers. Remember that unless you ask, people aren't likely to just jump in to help.

- *Contact*: On this page, you'll have a link that allows someone to send you an email. Also list a mailing address so someone can write a letter or send a contribution.

- *Events Calendar*: People want to know where you've been and where you'll be so that they can come to meet you. This list of events should be updated weekly so that people can make plans to meet you in person.

- *Press Releases, Clippings, and Media Links*: Post your own press releases to your website, together with fair-use excerpts and transcripts from and links to all the articles, photos, and television and radio interviews and debates that you want voters to see.

First and foremost, remember that your campaign website needs constant updating and monitoring. Treat anything that you post on your website as irrevocable: even material that you have deleted from your website may have been captured elsewhere, and it might resurface when you least expect it.

For an example of a campaign website as it looks in the final phase of a campaign, please visit my 2010 Idaho gubernatorial campaign website at www.JanaKemp.com/VoteKemp.

Decide How to Use Social Media

If you don't feel entirely comfortable with the term *social media*, now is the time to ramp up your curiosity and jump in. The use of social media made the difference in the 2008 presidential election, and it will affect race outcomes at every level now and into the future. *Social media* are web-based and mobile applications and services that are designed for the purpose of networking and socializing.

One hundred thirty-five years ago, the telephone was the first social medium to enter our culture because it allowed for two-way or multi-way conversations. Today, we have online communication tools that can be accessed through desktop computers at work and at home, and on laptops, tablets, and cell phones anywhere. This protean ability to access information and people instantly, anywhere, anytime, and across multiple platforms and devices is transforming social and networking patterns.

Your campaign opportunity, challenge, and imperative are to use social media in a way that gets your message in front of people you might not otherwise reach. Social media lets you "friend" and communicate with people. Social media expands your ability to point people to your campaign website, and, if you choose to, social media can help you field questions from voters and potential voters. There are dozens of social media sites and services. The most prominently used during the 2010, 2011, and 2012 election cycles are Facebook, Twitter, and LinkedIn. Social media have catalyzed such self-organizing grassroots political phenomena as the Tea Party and Occupy movements.

Use Facebook

Facebook, which launched in 2004, is a privately-owned social networking service and website. By the end of 2011, it had more than 800 million active users. By comparison, the world's biggest newspaper in 2011 had a circulation of fourteen million. Facebook is used as a social conversation tool, a business networking tool, a way to find long-lost friends and relatives, and a way to create shareable message boards and photo albums. Some people use Facebook as a dating tool. Still others use Facebook as a source for news, information, and political research.

You and your campaign team will want to set the ground rules for your campaign's use of Facebook. For example, who can post on your campaign page? Whom will you list as administrators (because you won't have time to keep up with this function) to oversee the site and monitor comments? How often will your team update the information on Facebook? What photos will you post? Will you link your Facebook comments to a Twitter account to reach even more potential voters?

Tweet Often on Twitter

Can you make your point in 140 characters or less? On Twitter, that's all you get. Share where you are. Post a provocative comment. Try it.

Join LinkedIn and Others

LinkedIn is a popular professional networking site. It allows messages in an email format to be sent. The site's format allows for a resume of work history to be entered. Whether you establish a campaign LinkedIn page and/or other social site campaign pages or not, people will look for you. Your not having a presence that at minimum says who you are, what you are running for and where to find your webpage will increasingly cost you votes. People want to find information in the places they frequently search without having to work too hard to find you and your campaign.

To expand your reach and name recognition, join as many social networking sites as you can and point everyone to your webpage. The reality is that you can't keep up with all social media outlets unless you have a team or a full-time person dedicated to the posting, monitoring, and response-prompting from you that this social networking effort demands.

Some social networking sites have advertising options. Most of the sites allow for a regional showing of the ads that lets you pick whom to show the ads to as your prospective voters. Some ad payment schemes are based on the placement of the ad; others are based on the click-through to your campaign website. Still others allow you to set a daily or monthly dollar amount that you are willing to spend and then the ad will no longer appear. Ask someone on your team to research the value of this to your campaign.

Use Email

You read in Chapter 8 about e-house parties for fundraising. Emails can be used to announce events, to communicate on a regular basis via newsletters, and to share news from your campaign. Emails are great for communicating with volunteers, too.

Newsletters via email require a constantly growing list of email addresses. You'll find companies that want to sell you email lists. You'll be approached by companies saying they'll send out your emails to their lists. Be skeptical. Ask lots of questions before deciding where to spend your advertising dollars with traditional, web-based, and social media outlets.

E-newsletters are a useful and time-effective way of communicating with voters, supporters, and contributors. Early in the campaign, the newsletter send-outs may happen weekly. As the campaign progresses toward the last month, you may determine that every two or three days you have enough information to share to excite voters to cast their ballots for you. Newsletter-worthy content includes the following:

- *News and Commentary:* Any time you issue a press release, you can include a shorter version in an e-newsletter. When you want to comment on a news item, you can do so in a campaign e-newsletter.

- *Your Campaign Website:* Always include your campaign website, so when readers forward your newsletter to friends, the friends can learn more about you and vote for you too.

- *Your Platform:* Include one of your platform statements in each newsletter. People want to know what you plan to do for them once you are in office. People can always go to your website to learn more.

- *Biographical Information*: People want to know who you are so they can figure out whether they relate to you and like you. Because this is a newsletter, include brief statements about your background and experience. People can always go to your website to learn more.

- *Invitation to Contribute*: Include the campaign contribution website link and a mailing address in every newsletter.

- *Invitation to Involved*: People want to be invited to participate in your campaign. Each newsletter you send gives you an opportunity to re-cruit volunteers.

- *Events Calendar*: People want to know where you'll be so that they can come to meet you. Update your event attendance announce-ments in every newsletter.

- *E-Fundraising Challenges*: A sample e-invitation to a fundraising event follows:

Dear Supporters of Jana Kemp for Governor,

Idaho is in need of great leadership. Jana Kemp is the independent and non-partisan leader we need for our economic and educational future.

INVITED: YOU, to be one of...

20 People – To the Table (Dinner Table that is) to talk with Jana Kemp about her run for 2010 Governor of Idaho.

WHAT:

We are holding a fundraising dinner with time to talk with Jana

- over a three-course catered meal
- and after-dinner world-class musical entertainment.

WHEN:

Wednesday, February 24.

6:00 p.m. until 9:00 p.m.

WHERE:

The Home of Bud and Elsie....

Cherry Lane in West Meridian (we'll provide directions when you RSVP!)

Contributions: $50 per person for this dinner event.

RSVP by February 16:

Reply to this email. Or, call: 208-***-****

I hope you will join us, in person, or by sending your support.

Can't Attend? Mail works as a good way to contribute!

Jana Kemp Governor 2010

PO Box 8045

Boise, ID 83707

Or feel free to get online to contribute: www.VoteKemp.com

Sincerely,

Jana Kemp

The Voice for Independent Idaho – because we need a Revolution of Good Government!

208-***-****

This email was prepared by Jana M. Kemp, LLC, and whoever forwarded the email to you. Feel free to forward this too!

▨ **Note** Twenty-first-century campaigns require an online and social media presence.

No Social Media in Motion?

With online and social media, you reach people who are no longer watching television or reading newspapers, and who, in the 2008 election cycle, overwhelmingly began to vote based largely on what they were learning online and at social media sites. Reach out to these young and/or technologically sophisticated voters. They may make the difference in your getting elected.

You must post to your social media at least weekly, and in some cases daily. You may not have time to do all of the posting. You and your campaign manager will want to identify one or two people who can help you monitor and post to social media sites. I found that having someone notify me when a social media posting required a response from me worked most effectively.

On occasion, you may find that certain people need to be banned from posting. You may also determine that you want to be the only one posting comments on your campaign social media pages. Remember that anything you post on your or anyone else's social media sites will exist in perpetuity. Remember that social media platforms reserve perpetual rights to all user content and will never permanently delete any data posted to sites, even after you've rejected or deleted it.

You may choose to sign up for social media lists, listservs, and e-newsletters. You and/or someone on your campaign team can also sign up for a variety of political, candidate, and event information. Stay abreast of what is happening by getting onto a variety of campaign and issue-related lists.

Using the Web as a Research Tool

Explore a variety of online resources that can help you expand your social media, political party and process, election, campaigning, and public service knowledge. The web is a powerful research tool that will also help you discover information about your challenger(s).

If your race's election date is more than six months away, you may find time to do some of this research yourself. However, if your race's election date is less than six months away, be sure to assign your campaign team members to do this research and present their findings to you. Here are some of the generic headings of online content, resources, and topics (rather than specific URLs, which can go rapidly out of date) which you should search for information relevant to your campaign:

- *Background Checks*: In some races, you may find that conducting background checks on individuals, potential staff and volunteer team members, or on other candidates is helpful. Spur-of-the-moment research from your mobile device works too. If you are in a meeting and need more information about someone else in that meeting, type in the person's name and see what comes up.

- *Blogs*: Discover who are the watchdogs and bloggers with large followings in your elected-office district. Tracking what is of interest and concern to people can help you define your position statements and responses to questions.

- *Campaign Consultants*: If you are feeling overwhelmed about managing a campaign, contact a campaign consultant to see what they recommend.

- *Campaign Literature*: This search will show you a variety of literature styles and content. See what you can learn from the ways other candidates have used campaign literature. It is also likely to show you which vendors can produce your campaign literature.

- *Campaign Media*: Look for tutorials and information on using the media, being interviewed, and working well with the media.

- *Campaign Plans/Political Strategies*: For more examples of campaign plans, conduct a search.

- *Campaign Schools*: Various colleges, non-profits, and political parties offer study programs for candidates and campaign workers.

- *Campaign Supplies*: From yard signs, bumper stickers and brochures to mailers, giveaways, and parade floats, you'll want to price your options.

- *Competitors' Campaign Websites*: Discover what others are saying about themselves—and maybe about you. Gather position statements and competitor intelligence.

- *Election Office(s)*: Research filing and reporting requirements and download forms. You can also research past elections to discover how many and where the votes fell for previous candidates.

- *Court Documents*: Many states have posted court records online. Use your state name and search terms "repository" or phrase "court documents." Typically you are taken to a court documents site and provided with an opportunity to type in someone's name. The names must match exactly for any information to appear. You may be surprised that what you learn is part of public record and available for anyone to find.

- *Events*: Fairs, parades, quilt shows, innovation fairs, tradeshows, agricultural events, community picnics, and other community events often have webpages of their own. Have a team member research what is happening and create a calendar of possible events where you can attend and shake hands.

- *Hard Money and Soft Money*: Continue to learn what the rules are and what options you may choose to pursue.

- *In-Kind Contributions*: Look for interesting contributions to jump-start your creativity in what you'll ask for as contributed services or items.

- *Interpersonal Communication*: Find books and articles that can help you strengthen your in-person presence, your presentation and debate skills, and your overall communication skills. Running for office is all about effective communication.

- *Issues*: You'll be amazed at the volume of information that a diligent search on any given campaign issue will turn up.

- *Newspapers*: Connect to as many newspapers as are covering the region of your race. Assisted by RSS feeds and Google Alerts, track coverage about yourself, others, issues, and hot topics of the day.

- *Political Fundraising*: There is an art and a science to political fundraising. Search for new ideas and for templates that may be helpful. Ask your campaign manager, treasurer, or fundraising chair to conduct research and make recommendations.

- *Political Messaging*: Online tutorials and historical documents can provide you with insights for your messaging. Remember to use only your own words.

- *Political Parties*: Monitor your county, state, and federal political party websites to learn what is happening in your race.

- *Political Position Statements*: Learn from others, but remember to always use your own words when describing your positions.

- *Political Use of Social Media*: The use of social media will increase as a tool for garnering votes. Learn how to best use social media by exploring online the best practices of candidates around the country.

- *Polling*: Online resources can tell you how to poll and provide information on companies that provide political polling services. Be very clear about the scope of work you expect to be accomplished, the fees and services, and the deadline by which you want to receive the information.

- *Radio and TV Stations*: Connect to as many stations as are covering the region of your race. Again, you can track coverage about yourself, others, issues, and hot topics of the day.

Conclusion

Whether or not you are enamored with the brave new world of social networking, you must get online to meet the people you might not ever see in person, might not shake hands with, and might not otherwise reach. In every community across America, the landscape for reaching voters has expanded to include online and social media. Grandparents are online so they can keep in contact with grandkids. Parents use online tools to manage work and to keep tabs on their kids. Campaigns use online tools and social media to reach voters. Get online!

Run: Work Face-to-Face

You have your campaign platform and message statements documented and available on information cards and at your website. You are about to embark on the most energy-consuming part of the campaign, meeting people face-to-face in a variety of settings. This chapter shares more of the campaign insights that will keep you smiling and shining brightly, earning votes every step and handshake of the way.

Take note of the questions posed, the tips offered, and the reminders in this chapter. You and your campaign team need to be in agreement about how to handle in-person meetings and events.

What You Wear Matters as Much as What You Say

Every event invitation is for a specific audience. Every event you attend has a specific purpose, whether it is a fair or a church-sponsored meet-the-candidate evening. Anticipating and adapting to the audience with whom you'll be meeting is important in the selection of your attire as well as in the preparation of your speech. If you wear disheveled clothing or dress inappropriately to your audience's sartorial expectations, they will infer that you are socially inept and not capable of doing the job for which you are running. Whatever you wear, be sure your clothes are clean, in good re-pair, and well pressed. Have extra shoes and clothes in your car in case you need to change.

Take into consideration the following tips and points of decorum when dressing yourself, your team, and your supporters for a campaign event:

- *Always Dress for the Position You Are Seeking*: If you are running for a position that requires suits, dress toward the more formal end of the continuum. If you are running for a position that allows business casual attire, then dress toward that style. Depending on the region of the country you are living in, your election district's expectations for formal and casual attire will vary. Dress accordingly.

- *Always Dress Appropriately to the Audience and Occasion*: At a fair, you might wear jeans with a pressed shirt or a campaign shirt with your logo. At a church event, match the attire worn by the congregation: is it church casual, suits and ties for men and dresses or skirts for women, or anything goes? For a backyard or home party atmosphere, dress a notch or two more professionally than the party hosts. Civic and business groups demand business attire that matches what they wear in formality or casualness.

- *Nametags*: You and your team members would do well to wear nametags since they invite public interaction and reinforce your name recognition. Nametag design is discussed elsewhere in this chapter.

- *Campaign Clothing*: T-shirts, collared shirts, jackets and hats with your campaign logo all fit into this category. If your campaign has the funds, create some clothing for yourself, your volunteers, and your supporters.

- *Campaign Buttons and Stickers*: These help spread the word and are wearable with anything. Plus, they are fairly inexpensive to produce.

- *Business Suits*: Meetings of business groups and formal presentations are usually suit-wearing events.

- *Business Casual*: Informal presentations, the fair and event circuit, and hosted events that indicate business casual is appropriate are the places to dress business casual.

- *Resort Wear*: Only dress this way when on a family vacation at a resort.

- *Casual Wear*: Only when an event host has indicated this is appro-priate should you consider it. Still, I'd wear business casual.

- *Beach Wear:* Avoid it. Enough said.

- *Church, Synagogue, or Mosque Attire:* This means a different style of clothing depending on the part of the country in which you live. No general style rule applies. Take into account each congregation's region, religion, denomination, as well as the nature of the event and your part in it. Have you been invited to deliver a talk, participate in a candidate forum, or to chat over coffee with a study group or community service group?

- *Western Wear:* Only wear this if you mean it and live it. I've owned cowboy boots for over three decades, so I wore them comfortably on the 2010 campaign trail around the state. I've never owned a cowboy hat, so never even put one on, despite running against men who were wrangling for the number-one cowboy title to be assigned to them during the race. Take into consideration where you live and how Western attire may help or hurt your candidacy.

- *Professorial Look:* If this is your natural style and fits the audience, you'll be fine. If you are faking it, your audience will know it.

- *Golf-Course Attire:* If you are on the golf course, dress accordingly. If you are not golfing, forgo the golf attire.

- *Shoes:* Take care of your shoes. Keep them polished. Select shoes that fit you well and in which you can stand and walk for hours. Your shoes should complement your attire and be comfortable.

- *Men and Women Get Treated Differently:* Sad but true. Women are still judged much more critically than men when it comes to clothing and accessories. Take your gender into account when choosing your clothing, jewelry, accessories, and shoes. After one of my debates, a campaign volunteer reported having heard that someone thought my pearls were too big. I was disgusted but not surprised. I bet this same person didn't even notice the color of the male candidates' ties or the size of their cufflinks, much less criticize them. Men, you can dress professionally in clean and well-maintained clothes and, as long as your attire fits the occasion, you'll be in good shape. Women, you must take more care, spending more time and putting more thought into matching your outfits and accessories to the audience. Be prepared to receive comments that men will never hear about their clothing, and gracefully say something like "thank you for sharing" in a tone that is kind and gracious.

- *Television and Advertising Shoots:* When dressing for cameras, select clothing that will be flattering to you. For instance, busy prints, solid blue or solid green (because these colors are used for photographic overlays in television), fabrics with many colors, and large-weave tweeds can make cameras lose focus and make you appear fuzzy or larger than you may be. Watch what other candidates and incumbents wear. You'll begin to notice that they are primarily wearing solid colors that work well in any setting.

Make the Most of Your Personality and Intelligence

You are who you are. Know enough about yourself, your strengths, and your personal challenges that you can make the most of who you are when campaigning. Here are some personality types and traits you should watch for in yourself, so that you can hone your face-to-face skills accordingly:

- *Everyone Is Not You*: It seems obvious, but it is important to remember that people are not just variations on your own basic personality. Some people want details, whereas others just want key points. Some people want to listen to you, whereas others just want you to listen to them. Some people want to know you are nice, whereas others want to know you are competent. Some people want you to believe in God, preferably theirs, and other people don't care what god you believe in. Everyone is not like you.

- *Introvert*: You'd prefer not to have to meet a room full of people.

- *Extrovert*: You love meeting people—bring 'em on!

- *Knowledgeable*: You are smart, bookish, community-knowledgeable, and able to answer any question at any time. Some people may be impressed. Others may be skeptical that anyone can know this much about so many things.

- *Talkative*: You talk more than you listen. You might even interrupt others when they are speaking.

- *Listener*: You listen more than you talk. You might find that people tell you things you would never disclose to strangers.

- *Complainer*: You're running because you're mad and want changes, yet you come across as a complainer who is not offering solutions.

- *Problem-Solver*: You're running because you see solutions and want to implement improvements.

- *Attacker*: You are running because the incumbent is not doing the job and you want him or her out of office. You come out swinging more often than not, trying to prove how unfit the incumbent is for the job.

- *Victim*: You've been hurt and you want yourself and others to stop being hurt. You can come across as a problem-solver or as a complainer, depending on the ideas you offer and the approach you take with your campaign messages.

- *Victimizer*: You believe all people should be self-reliant and that government should never provide help to the needy under any circumstances. When you stay in an angry mindset, you are coming across as a victimizer. Be aware of the impact you are having on others.

- *Passionate, hot-button-issue-driven*: One issue caused you to enter the race. It is all you talk about. Remember from Chapter 7 the Idaho man who legally changed his name to Mr. Pro-Life, because this is his hot-button topic and the sole reason he runs for office, year after year after year?

Reflect upon the display of personality and intelligence you bring to every meeting. Will you capitalize on your strengths, or will you let your inner strengths turn into outer weaknesses when meeting people face-to-face? Remember to end every conversation with "I look forward to earning your vote" or "Thanks for your vote" or "I'm glad to have earned your vote." You want people to remember what you are asking for, and that is their vote for you.

Work a Room

For introverts, the most exhausting part of a campaign is working rooms, meeting people, walking a fair circuit, and telling the same story briefly and repeatedly. For extroverts, meeting people is the most exhilarating part of the campaign.

Whatever your personality, map out for yourself how you will successfully work a room. Here are some of the many points of etiquette to consider when working a room:

- *Be appropriate*: If it is not your event, don't make the event about you. Respect the event and the event hosts. You can discreetly and appropriately introduce yourself and your candidacy to others.

- *Introductions*: Use a standard single-line self-introduction: "Hello, I'm Jana Kemp and I'm running for governor this year;" or, "Hello, I'm John Smith and I'm running for the school board."

- *Handshakes*: Shake each person's hand like you are happy to meet him or her, not too firmly and not too softly. Practice this if you have any doubts about the sincerity and appropriateness of your handshake.

- *Food*: If the event host has indicated food has been provided for you, be gracious and accept. The general rule is that you should provide or buy your own food. In most cases, you will be so busy meeting people that you will not have time to eat. So, eat before the event begins or after the event ends.

- *Nametags*: People should know who you are and who is on your campaign team. Go to a trophy company or print shop to get pin or magnetic nametags made. Choose a color and shape that represents your campaign and the seat for which you are running. For instance, I chose a blue nametag with white letters in the shape of the state, because blue and white were campaign colors and I was running for a statewide office.

- *Standing vs. sitting*: Here's the rule: once you sit down, you will be engaged in a longer conversation than if you stay standing or even if you kneel down beside someone to talk. Use your best judgment about standing or sitting. Generally, you'll want to stay standing so that you can gracefully close a conversation and move on to meet new people.

- *Podium etiquette*: If you are invited to speak from a podium, use the microphone, be brief, and be sure to thank the event host for giving you a moment to introduce yourself. Do not—I repeat, do not—be a podium hog or long-winded, because you'll lose votes.

- *Be gracious*: Some people may walk right past you without realizing that you are running for office. Be patient and gracious as you take a moment to introduce yourself. At one event where I and a male campaign volunteer were working, people kept approaching him (because he was a man) as the candidate. He would graciously direct them to me as the candidate. At that point I would smile, extend my hand for a handshake and introduce myself. The only person who can knock you out of the running in a situation like this is you. Respond graciously, share your message, and ask for the vote or say "I'd like to earn your vote."

- *Safety and Security—Yours*: You, your campaign team, and any additional hired security personnel need to have an exit plan for every place you go. Never walk alone. Always have a cell phone with you to be able to dial 9-1-1 for yourself or others in need of help. If you travel to an event in a marked car, determine what type of threat or disturbance that could endanger you will cause you to leave the event. Then determine whether you will leave in the same vehicle or an unmarked vehicle (which is what I recommend). Hopefully you'll never need to implement a safety plan. However, you are best served and will have a greater peace of mind if you have a safety plan in place.

- *Safety and Security—Others*: If your presence is creating a safety issue for others, leave quickly and gracefully. There are times when your presence at an event may draw so much attention that others are endangered. You and your team need to be aware of your impact on others and act accordingly to protect others.

Make a Speech

You've been invited to a social group, a civic club, a business group, a religious group, or a school. You are expected to make a speech of three to fifteen minutes. What will you say?

You and your team will be best served if you craft two or three standard speeches that can be tailored to each audience that invites you to speak. You do after all have your campaign platform and message statements; they are in your candidate information and on your website. Be prepared to make a great professional presentation. Consider these general speech-making pointers:

- *Script*: Again, you will be best served if you and your team craft two or three standard speeches that can be tailored to each audience to whom you are invited to speak. Some candidates prefer to read their speeches while maintaining eye contact. Others memorize their speeches word for word. Still others of us memorize the key points and extemporize our speeches based on immediate audience needs and interests. Whatever your preference, be able to give a speech at any moment, to any audience.

- *Podiums*: If there is a podium, use it. You don't have to stand behind it the whole time as long as your audience can hear you when you move away from the podium. Keep your hands off the sides of the podium. Thumping or clutching the podium makes you appear pompous or nervous. Resting your hands on the top of the podium, or using your hands to move the pages of your speech, is just fine.

- *Microphones*: If a microphone is available, use it. Don't say, "Oh my voice is loud enough." Your job is to protect your voice for the long haul of the campaign. Your job is to make sure that people can hear you without straining. One of the best public speaking tips I've ever gotten came from a college job in Minnesota. This is the tip: step up to the microphone, take a silent breath, and speak calmly to the whole audience, including the person in the last row who is wearing a hearing aid. Everyone in the room must hear you to have a good experience.

- *Pockets*: Keep change and your hands out of your pockets. Putting your hands in your pockets while speaking in public suggests nervousness or concealment. Fidgeting distracts your audience from what you are saying.

- *Q&A*: Be gracious when fielding questions. Listen to the whole question. Repeat the question as concisely and accurately as you can. Repeating the question allows you to restate a rambling or incoherent question so that you can answer it in a way that relates to you and your platform. It also gives you time to formulate your best answer. Offer your response, then move politely to the next questioner.

Participate in a Debate

Track what groups and media outlets are planning debates. Get yourself invited to, and attend, every debate and candidate forum for your seat that you can. Not all debate and forum sponsors will invite you, so be sure to politely position yourself as a viable candidate and get yourself invited. Complete all participation criteria forms accurately and in detail. Keep track of your campaign activities and fundraising so you can report this information when asked for it by debate organizers.

Consider these general debating pointers:

- *Do Your Homework*: Study your position statements and know them forwards and backwards. Have supporting information at your fingertips. Study your issues logs to remind yourself of what your challengers have said and committed to accomplishing.

- *Be Nice*: Understand the rules of the debate, all of which impose time limits on speakers. Know who the timekeeper is and where he or she will be sitting. Use all your allotted time without sounding long-winded. Respect the moderator, even if he or she is doing a poor or biased job. Respect your challengers and demonstrate your leadership capacities.

- *Speak Clearly and Calmly*: Show what you know. Demonstrate that you are approachable and that you care about people and their concerns. Tell slice-of-life stories from voters to support your points. Talk about what you learned going door-to-door or meeting people at fairs. Be clear and succinct in your responses to questions.

- *Be Agile*: Know that debate organizers do not usually give you their questions in advance. You must be prepared for anything and everything. Increasingly in televised and social-networked debates, moderators feed live tweeted, emailed, and video-Skyped questions into the debate.

Debates are your opportunity to showcase your whole candidate package: character, integrity, knowledge, accuracy, compassion, personality, humor, dignity, style, composure, and passion. Be so thoroughly prepared that you can relax and be yourself. Get coaching to improve your presentation and delivery, and remember to smile.

Work the Fair or Event Circuit

A great way to reach large numbers of people is to go to where people gather. Most fairs will rent booths to political candidates and/or parties. And fairs and events usually have seating areas, food vendors, and space to wander. These fair and event spaces are a great place to say hello, introduce yourself, shake hands, hand out a flyer, and ask for votes.

A master of the fair circuit during election years was U.S. Congressman Walt Minnick (D-Idaho). He traveled with a volunteer team wearing Minnick shirts and brandishing Minnick literature. He genuinely smiled, listened, and shook hands like he'd known you his whole life. He continues to interact with people like he really cares, because he does. He worked harder than any other U.S. elected official I've seen in person.

What do you want people to remember about their interactions with you? "Talk less, listen more" is a good personal reminder for fairs, events, and going door to door.

Create Your Own Event Circuit

You and your campaign can create a fundraising and meet-the-candidate circuit of your own. Determine whether your potential contributors and voters will come to special-invitation events to meet you in person and support the campaign financially. Consider that one of the benefits of holding events is that the event is happening and you can invite people—this form of endorsement by the event holder and host and your ability to announce it is a benefit to your campaign. The bigger benefit comes from having people in attendance who will contribute. Several people may host your campaign events; the more high-profile your hosts are in your election district, the more likely others are to sign on to help your campaign. Be sure the event hosts listed on each invitation attend the events to help with the fundraising.

Recall from Chapter 6 that campaign-hosted events are a part of your campaign plan. Hold at least five events before determining whether to schedule more or whether to discontinue the effort. Continue holding the events if people are showing up, asking questions that are beneficial to them and to you, and are making financial contributions. Stop holding the campaign-specific events and pursue other types of outreach to voters and contributors when the events are not proving to be worth the effort.

Go Door-to-Door

Going door-to-door is a time- and energy-consuming task. It is a great way to learn about your district. In city council and county commission races, voters still expect to meet you in person. The bigger the territory of your district, the lower the expectation of voters to meet you on their doorsteps.

Over the course of the last twenty or thirty years, finding people at home has become more difficult. Focus your and your team's walking time on the parts of the district where you know registered voters live and at times when you know they are most likely to be home. Remember, you can get registered voter addresses and, sometimes, voter addresses filtered by political party, from your election office.

Here are some tips about going door-to-door:

- *Chatty people*: Some people will want to talk and talk and talk. Prepare some phrases that you can use to show respect but excuse yourself so that you can move on to the next door. For example: "Thank you for having such great concern for our community. I do, too. That's why I'm running. I'll share this card with you so that you can reach me by email or by mail to share your concerns."

- *Hospitable people:* Be careful about accepting an invitation to go inside the house. Don't go in unless you're traveling in a pair or someone else on your team knows exactly where you are. Consider going in only if you know the person well. Limit your time, or you could find yourself in a person's home for hours, yet still not earn the vote. The safest policy is just to set a campaign rule: "Never go in."

- *Dogs:* Always be aware that a dog could be in the yard, in a garage, or about to come out of the house. Protect yourself by not entering a property where a dog is present. Be prepared if a vicious dog suddenly appears. If a friendly dog is circling you to be petted, ask the owner if you may pet the dog, and then, pet the dog, or you really will be less likely to earn the owner's vote.

- *Fences:* If a yard is fenced, there is a reason. Don't enter a fenced yard unless you have been invited.

- *Walking on grass:* Don't do it. Respect people's property. Ask flyer delivery teams to respect people's property. Use sidewalks and driveways to get to front doors.

- *Mailboxes:* Don't use them. Mailboxes are the property of the U.S. Postal Service. Candidates can be fined for flyers left in or on mailboxes. The only candidate pieces to go into mailboxes are the ones you have paid the U.S. Postal Service to mail for you.

- *"No Soliciting" signs:* Use your best judgment about whether to leave a flyer or not. Definitely don't ring the doorbell unless you know who lives there.

- *Always leave a flyer:* Whether you speak to a person or not, leave a flyer. Write "sorry to miss you" and sign your first name when leaving a flyer at an unanswered door.

- *Door slamming in your face:* This happens rarely. Don't take it personally. Someone else's rudeness should not throw you off course. In fact, you can smile to yourself and thank your lucky stars that this person has saved you time for people who really may vote for you.

- *Travel in pairs:* Whether you are a man or a woman, your safest door-to-door strategy is to travel in pairs. This way you and your volunteers always have an immediate ear to respond for help in the event help is needed.

- *Hiring flyer delivery or using volunteer delivery teams:* This helps you to cover more ground than you could cover by yourself. Have street maps printed and then highlight the streets where the most voters live, so that teams can concentrate on most-likely voters. You can also assign teams to high-density housing developments or apartment buildings. Remember to get permission for flyer deliveries when necessary.

- *Nursing homes and care facilities with voting and absentee voting coordinators*: Our elder citizens vote. In some districts like mine, which had ten care facilities and only 38,000 potential voters, these facilities can decide the election outcome. Get flyers into residents' hands. Give a presentation and answer questions at the facilities that will allow you to come onsite.

While door-to-door campaigning is time consuming, it is also a great way to learn about your district and your potential voters. Put door-to-door time on your campaign calendar. Enlist volunteers to go with you, and enlist volunteers to go out in teams to delivery flyers without you.

On-the-Spot, Impromptu Meetings

While running errands, you may meet voters. When you fill your tank with gas, someone may approach you to ask a question. While you are driving, people are watching you, how you drive and how well they think you will lead based on your driving habits. While you are grocery shopping, returning library books, banking, or doing shopping of any kind, potential voters may approach you to ask a question, share an insight, or simply to make a comment.

When I was first considering a run for office in 2004, a mayor I had met at a Louisville conference at which I had spoken was the first person I called to ask about what it is like to hold elected office. I called someone out of state because I wasn't yet ready to tip my hand in state. The mayor was the first to describe in detail how much of your personal life can be lost to others who will approach you at any time, in any place. She went on to make clear that your family is as much a part of the elected-office experience as you are, because they, at the very least, will have to spend a lot of time waiting for you while you talk with people you know and people you are meeting for the first time in impromptu encounters.

Be prepared for these impromptu meetings. You might be pleasantly surprised or alarmed by who approaches you and for what reasons they want to talk with you. When leaving an event, people might approach you on the street or in a parking lot or parking garage. Your job is to remain alert and to be responsive to the person or people who have approached you to engage. On the stay-alert front, be aware of the times that you may want to have 9-1-1 pre-dialed on your cell phone so that all you have to do is press call/send and have help on the way.

Sparring with Opponents

This is a personal style choice. Campaign consultants may advise you to spar and attack. You don't have to. It is your campaign and you get to choose the tone, tenor, and style with which you will conduct the campaign.

Will you spar? Or will you steer clear of sparring? If you choose to spar, prepare yourself to be attacked, particularly if you are an incumbent. Shouting until you turn red does you no good. It may get you onto television, YouTube, and into rebroadcasted news stories, but you'll be likely to lose the race.

Good-natured, humorous bantering can work, as long as listeners do not perceive it as an attack. I've seen candidates use biting humor, which I think only demeans the person using it and can lead to attacking behavior. In their 1988 vice-presidential debate, Democratic candidate Senator Lloyd Bentsen famously responded to Republican candidate Senator Dan Quayle's self-comparison to John F. Kennedy: "Senator, I served with Jack Kennedy; I knew Jack Kennedy; Jack Kennedy was a friend of mine. Senator, you're no Jack Kennedy." Although Bentsen scored a debate zinger, his ticket lost the election by an eight percent margin. By contrast, Republican presidential candidate Ronald Reagan's 1992 spoof on Bentsen's sarcasm was well-received across the political spectrum, because he good-naturedly directed it against himself as well as his Democratic opponent, Bill Clinton: "This fellow they've nominated claims he's the new Thomas Jefferson. Well, let me tell you something. I knew Thomas Jefferson. He was a friend of mine. And Governor, you're no Thomas Jefferson."

Responding to Attacks

Don't get pulled into a fight. Hold your ground, report your truths, state the facts, and present your platform. Never stoop to recriminations or name-calling. Instead of calling your opponent a liar, dispute the veracity of his statement: "That is not true. The truth is...." Transition smoothly to share something positive from your platform. Don't give more attention to an attack than it merits. Don't get bogged down in defense and counterattack. Instead, be a leader, which is why you are asking for people's votes.

Will it be hard? Yes. Will you master your impulses and stay out of the fray? Hopefully so. Enlist your trusted inner-circle campaign team members to simulate debate situations with you, so that you can rehearse appropriate responses to inflammatory remarks and falsehoods.

When you are alone in the moment and cameras are rolling, take a breath, gather your thoughts, smile, and calmly speak the truth. (I find it restores my sense of proportion to remember one of my favorite movie lines: "I never did mind about the little things much.") If an attack is so flagrantly negative and mean-spirited that it boomerangs on the attacker, consider not even dignifying it with a response. Instead move on to your point and offer your vision and solutions for what the elected position and the community needs. The audience will draw its own conclusions about which candidate they'd rather see in office.

Recovering from Gaffes and Mistakes

Be able to laugh at yourself if you make a mistake. Be able to admit you were wrong if you were wrong, and carefully craft your admission statement. Always own it and take responsibility. Blaming a staffer or volunteer makes you appear weak and lacking in leadership skills. People want to see and experience you as a capable leader.

During a campaign, you are thrust into dozens of unexpected situations. The chances that somewhere along the way you will commit a gaffe or make a mistake are high. Anticipate this and be ready to roll with the punches, let the water roll off your back, and get right back up in the saddle. Whatever phrase or metaphor you use to coach yourself through an embarrassing moment, get through it with honesty, humility, and humor and move on.

Making the Most of Volunteers

While you work a room, volunteers can too. Volunteers can give out literature. Volunteers can help shield you from talkative constituents. Volunteers can help collect contributions from supporters so you can stay focused on meeting people, listening to their concerns, and shaking hands.

Before each event, talk with your volunteers about what role(s) you want them to play. Ask them to wear campaign colors, shirts with logos, and/or campaign nametags. You want the people in the room to know who is with you and who is already supporting the campaign.

Be sure to thank volunteers throughout the campaign for their efforts. While you can do this online, many volunteers still prefer in-person election night parties and handwritten thank you notes.

The Last Days of the Campaign

The last week of a campaign is the most grueling. You are tired from all of the work you've already done. People have asked questions you'd never imagined. Media has been kind or rough on you. Either way, you're exhausted. The majority of candidates I've talked to agree that in the last week of the campaign, they're so exhausted that they just want it to be over, and don't even care anymore about the outcome, which of course is not true.

You must be forearmed for a frenzied round of activities, events, and contingencies in the final phase of your campaign. Eleventh-hour activities and events to expect from others include the following:

- *Televised debates*: Debates can happen at any time. However, the televised debates in non-presidential elections usually run in the final month and days of an election. Be sure to get onto the debates.

- *Candidate Summaries in Newspapers and Online*: You will have already responded to the surveys from newspapers, yet candidate responses don't end up running in newspapers until the last days of a campaign.

- *Last-minute mudslinging mailings*: In my 2004 race for state representative, I had been told that the Democrat running against me always sent a final-weekend mailer slamming his opponent. Knowing this, my campaign made sure that our final mailed postcard highlighted my strengths and what I would do. My goal was to stay positive and to counteract his mud-slinging. It worked, as did the whole of that campaign: I was elected.

- *Mud-slinging in partisan blogs and radio and television attack-ads*: Sometimes these tactics begin before the race nears its end. Sometimes challengers will wait until the last few days, hoping that you won't have time to respond or counteract their messages about you. Research your opponents' practices and plan how you will handle their campaign tactics against you.

What to expect of yourself in the final days of your campaign:

- *You'll be tired*: If you haven't done all you can do before this week, knocking yourself out now won't matter. Take care of yourself.

There will be another day, another race, and another opportunity no matter the outcome of this particular election.

- *Stay professional*: Even though you are tired, don't let your guard down. Candidates have done themselves in by letting their guard down in the final days and hours of a campaign.

- *Be gracious and thankful*: Your volunteers, contributors, and voters cheered, worked, contributed, and voted for you and your campaign. Be sure to thank them for their support, regardless of whether you win or lose. If your election funds are exhausted, send your thank you notes electronically. If you have any remaining funds, mailed thank you notes are classy.

■ **Note** Work the room, the restaurant, the fair, the sidewalk, and the stairway. Everyone needs to know you are in the race, and they are happier when they can say "I met him/her."

Didn't Work the Crowd? You've Made It Hard to Win

If you didn't reach out in person, voters didn't get to see you as a real person. Be sure to schedule yourself into face-to-face events throughout your campaign. In fact, former Michigan governor James Blanchard told me, "You need to attend three to four good events a day, in person, to win." When running in a smaller election district, you need at least one good in-person event per day. People want to see you in person and judge your character. Can they like you and trust you? They'll make that assessment from every aspect of your campaign, but never more forcefully than when they meet you in person.

Will they vote for you? You can never know for sure. But shaking people's hands and looking them in the eye sure increases your odds.

Conclusion

While seated at a dinner table many years ago with former Kentucky Governor Martha Layne Collins, I saw firsthand her vision and passion for her state, even though her term as governor had ended a decade prior. I could see and feel with every sentence she offered to those of us around the table how she won the Toyota Plant for Kentucky. Her graciousness radiated warmth, her knowledge and tenacity presented a can-do spirit, and her depth of care for the people of her state rang true.

The face-to-face connections you make are fleeting. I only met Martha Layne Collins once and yet she left a positive and permanent impression on me. Your face-to-face time will be remembered through Election Day, or possibly for a lifetime. Be kind, intelligent, gracious, truthful, and passionate throughout your campaign.

You built your plan, set your budget, got yourself in front of the media, managed your mailing and email lists, communicated via social media, maximized your online and traditional media outreach, and worked as many rooms and shook as many hands as you could. All these efforts should lead to a win.

Win

Congratulations! You've won! All of your hard work has paid off. You are the officeholder-elect. Once you are sworn in, you will be holding the position you worked so hard to achieve. Take a breath—a quick one—and celebrate.

Now the real work begins. Holding elected office involves at minimum one and as many as four jobs: the elected-office job, the job you may still work to keep your household bills paid, the job of ongoing campaigning, and the job of being a household family member. Your work must clearly differentiate the elected job from the ongoing campaign job, if you plan to run for re-election.

Time management, work prioritization, and setting and sticking to firm boundaries are critical to performance in office. In order to keep work and family balanced, one elected official I met confided: "I only allow myself to be scheduled into meetings until 7:00 p.m. Then, I go home so that I can spend the evening with my family." With a work day that started at 7:00 a.m., twelve hours for her elected job seemed a reasonable daily limit to her.

Be Prepared for the Responsibility That Falls on Your Shoulders

You've officially taken office. Your realm of responsibility has just been enlarged. You still have your life and family responsibilities. You still have your campaign team and reporting responsibilities. Now, you have all of the responsibilities of being an elected official to add to your daily list of considerations and concerns. Some of the responsibilities that apply to every elected office are the following:

Budget Setting and Oversight: Every elected office is responsible for some level of budgeting research, recommendation, and review. Whether you have staff support in legions, or minimal research and number-crunching support, the ultimate responsibility for budget setting and holding the line on budgets rests with you.

Constituent and Stakeholder Interactions: Letters, emails, scheduled and impromptu meetings, and phone calls will demand your time and attention. The more visible the position you hold, the more time you'll spend with other people. The more controversial the topics of an elected position are, the more information you'll receive from people about their ideas for what you should do and the more time you'll find yourself listening to others about what they think you should do. For instance, positions dealing with zoning, pet control, education, water, land, and life-and-death issues attract heavy constituent comment and input.

Law, Rule, Policy Creation, and Oversight: Every elected office has a job component tied to setting new ideas into motion and to refining work that is already underway. This happens through the creation of laws, codes, rules, ordinances, and policies. In legislative branch positions, formal votes are needed, so in addition to committee meetings and work sessions, the proposed changes will be brought to you at an official, on-the-record, vote-holding meeting. In judicial, law enforcement, and executive branch positions rule and policy creation and oversight is also a part of the elected office job.

Meeting Attendance: Some elected offices are subject to a miss-too-many policy, which penalizes chronic inattendance with the loss of office. Most elected offices do not have a must-attend meetings rule. Attend official meetings anyway.

Questions: Asking and answering questions are duties, not options. Failing to ask questions leads to misinformation, incomplete information, and eventually to job failure. Failing to answer questions will quickly get you branded as rude, ignorant, or arrogant—which are qualities that may lead your constituents to recall you.

What Can You Expect on the Job

In addition to the responsibilities that fall on your shoulders, there are a variety of activities and expectations that will consume your time, your mind, and your family's time:

Calendars: Even before you are sworn in, you'll begin getting mail, email, and invitations to events. Your calendar will be full before you know it. I found that putting all my life's events onto one calendar was critical, so that no calendar conflicts occurred and nothing fell apart. I also found that taking time to record invitations on my calendar for events that I was specifically invited to attend required twice-a-week attention and responses. Taking time to review my schedule was critical to keeping on top of what I could and could not realistically attend.

Committee Assignments: Every elected position ends up being assigned to committees. Some of the committees will be internal to the board, commission, or agency you are serving. (Note: in government-speak, the word *agency* refers to the entity which you serve, whether it be the departments that report to the governor or the mayor; the offices that report to the sheriff or commissioners; the department as a whole under an elected official; the districts or entities that are beholden unto themselves and their elected commissions or boards; and generally to any entity that is not otherwise referred to as a council, commission, or board.) On other committees and councils you will represent your agency to other agencies. On yet other committees, you will represent your agency among business, industry, union, and trade association groups. Some of the committees will be task forces and time-limited in nature. Others will be long-standing committees for which you become one in a venerable succession of elected officials. Before I accept a committee assignment, I always ask: "What is this committee tasked with doing and what am I expected to contribute?" Again, your calendar will be full before you can blink, so stay on top of scheduling and your calendar.

Endorsements: Because you won the election, you are a winner in everyone's eyes for at least the length of your current term. Other candidates for office in following years may ask for your endorsement. Party members may ask for your endorsement for jobs they are pursuing, or for elections they plan to enter. Check with your elections office to see what is legal in your state. Check with party officials to see what is acceptable and what is against party policy. Sometimes nonprofit organizations will ask you to serve on their boards and advisory boards; saying "yes" becomes an endorsement of the organization. So, do your homework to be sure that you are committing to a sound organization that is indeed serving the community, is well managed, and will not cause you heartache or a loss of political standing. On occasion people with products or services will ask for your testimonials—all I can say is be careful and check what laws govern commercial endorsement by public officials in your state and on the federal level.

Hours: You set your hours. I repeat: you are in control of the hours you commit to working. Will you work a ten-hour, twelve-hour, or fourteen-hour day? Five, six, or seven days a week? You set the rules and the boundaries.

Stick to them, and the people around you will begin to honor your hours. If you let people have access to you all of the time, you will rarely get any time for yourself, or any uninterrupted time with your family.

Learning New Things Daily: For some people, the daily mix of discussion, research, and presentation on all manner of topics is exciting, exhilarating, and enormously satisfying. For other people, those same demands may induce feelings of exhaustion, chaos, and oppression or even depression. The volume of things to learn, analyze, evaluate, and synthesize never diminishes. Once you have the big picture, you have to keep abreast of the relentless torrent of details that go with your committee and budgetary work.

Laws, Policies and Procedures, Rules and Regulations, Codes and Covenants: Yes, these are all things you must understand. You must know what they are, how they are different, and what the process is for making one and for enforcing one. You must know who makes the law, policy, rule, or code and whom to call for enforcement. Constituents will ask you about both the making and the enforcement of nearly everything. You may end up digesting nuances and legalities on a gamut of issues from weed control to capital punishment.

Meetings: More meetings than you can presently imagine are heading into your life. If you've held office before, you have a sense of how quickly meetings can devour your time. The key question to ask before committing to a meeting is the same as the one you should ask before accepting a committee appointment: "What is the purpose of the meeting and what do you want/need from me as a result of my attendance?" Sometimes people will be straightforward. Most of the time you'll discover that the meeting-holders or meeting-callers have not been asked this question before. As a result, there may be some stammering followed by a phrase such as "Your predecessor always came" or "We'd really like to have you come." Be selective as to which meetings and groups you choose. Be sure that you will benefit from sharing information, and collaborating on solutions to problems that matter to your constituents.

Meeting Protocols: Do you know how to address the chair? Are you primed on the proper protocol for asking a question? Do you know how to make and withdraw motions? Do you know how to get information into and out of the minutes? Find a mentor who can guide you through this political minefield. This knowledge and skill will help you immensely.

Parliamentary Procedure: Does your elected position rely on Mason's or Robert's Rules of Order? These are the most-often used parliamentary guides. In some positions, there are additional parliamentary documents that you should receive when being sworn in. However, you may have to ask.

Paperwork: You are serving in a branch of government, so it goes without saying that you'll see paperwork, touch paperwork, and create paperwork on a daily basis. Figure out what must be kept and filed, what can be destroyed, and what is subject to public records requests. Most administrative staff in your agency can help you figure this out.

Party Fundraising Expectations: Remember, now you are considered a winner in the world of politics. The act of running didn't make you a winner. Winning made you a winner. So, if you ran as a political party candidate, now the party wants a piece of you, your time, your campaign money, and your personal money. Find out quickly what is expected, or set your own boundaries and live up to them.

People, Lots of People: Nearly every part of an elected official's job requires interacting face-to-face with people. The only solitary work you have is reading your piles of paper documents or email inbox, and responding to constituent letters. Even then you'll find yourself interrupted by people walking in or phone calls. If you still weren't used to being around people by the end of the campaign, it's time to get used to being around and working with people.

Politics and Political Maneuvering: Pay attention to what is happening around you, what happens during committee meetings, in the hallways, during voting, and in seemingly unrelated meetings. Intrigue, arm-twisting, and deal-cutting are daily possibilities. Politics is a sticky, ego-filled business. Elected officials and the teams of people supporting them generally have outsized egos that can cause them to be seduced from public service by political posturing. Beware.

At one point while serving as a state representative, I was sponsoring an economic development bill at the same time that I was opposing an education reform bill that would have had adverse budget and staffing implications. A person working for the governor approached me in a capitol building hallway and said something that sounded like, "If you want the governor to sign your econ[omy] bill, you need to change your vote on the education reform bill." Shocked, I said: "Are you threatening me? Because I happen to know for a fact that the governor wants the econ[omy] bill I'm sponsoring." Of course, the curt reply was a "no" headshake.

A week later, in another impromptu hallway meeting, I asked the governor's chief of staff whether it was the governor's policy to twist legislators' arms. To his airy dismissal—"No, that's just politics"—I replied: "No, politics is knowing what I want and knowing what you want and figuring out a way for everyone to get what he/she wants while serving the public good."

Public Information and Public Record: You are an elected official, which means everything you say and do is under public scrutiny. As an elected official, everything you do and say that is related to your elected position becomes public information, which means it can be subject to public record requests. Your emails, letters, committee notes, committee minutes, and voicemails can all potentially be requested through public record requests. So, check the applicable laws and your agency's policies to become clear about what becomes public. When in doubt, be transparent.

Reading: Need I say more? You are by now well aware that you will be reading mountains of information during your elected service. Buy your highlighting pens in bulk.

Staff: Discover immediately what, if any, staff support you will have as an elected official. Determine what tasks you will do and which tasks you'll delegate. Learn how staff members prefer to receive information, requests, and assignments. For instance, do they prefer emails, telephone calls, in-person conversations, or spoken directions with supporting visual examples? Remember to be respectful to all staff members. Without them you won't accomplish much. Without earning their respect, you can count on the staff-room conversations including things that are not respectful toward you. Everyone talks at work and in her social circles. You are on view at all times, especially with staff members.

Voting: If you are an elected official, you will cast votes or render decisions. Here's what you need to know: Your votes and decisions are a matter of public record. Ask whether you must cast a "yes" or "no" vote or whether you may abstain while sitting at the table. Ask whether you must leave the room in order to avoid casting a vote. Discover whether you can have someone else sit in your seat and cast a vote on your behalf. Learn what the paired-voting rules are, if your entity has any. Learn what the parliamentary procedure is for your entity so that you can understand the nuances of debate and vote casting. Be the master of your vote, rather than depending on the mercy of the people around you. Always know why you have cast a vote in the way that you have. Someone may ask you at the gas pump why you voted the way you did.

One of my favorite vote-casting stories concerns the time I voted "no" on a constitutional amendment to ban gay marriages in the state. Whatever your beliefs about this, keep reading. The constitutional amendment, which passed, affirms that "one man can marry one woman." But the terms "man" and "woman" are not defined in the Idaho Code. This ambiguity means that a woman who has had a sex change to become a man is free under Idaho's amended constitution to marry a man who has had a sex change to become a woman. However one rates the efficacy of sex change operations, the hypothetical couple either still has or has ended up with opposite sexual poles: one is a man and the other is a woman. Every time I explain this legal nuance to people, their mouths drop open in shock, amusement, or delight, depending on their personal values and orientations.

I repeat, know how the vote-casting process works in your elected position and always know why you voted the way you did. People are watching, and people will ask. Your future challengers are keeping count and tracking your comments so that they can use your votes and comments against you.

What Can You Expect in Your Personal Life?

All of the on-the-job demands described in this chapter mean that your personal life is also changed. Some elected officials lose control of their calendars, thereby surrendering control of their social and personal lives. Most are able to reserve some personal time.

Here are some of the repercussions you can expect in your personal life after winning elected office:

Less Time with Your Family: If your family already wasn't seeing much of you, maybe they won't notice the difference. However, most families do notice that you are home less, talking to other people more, and generally more tired than before you won.

Continual Interruptions When You Are Out in Public: If your race was well covered by the media, you will continue to be noticed when you're out and about in your private life. I've been approached by strangers at the supermarket, the gas station, the car wash, restaurants, and the movies. People usually want to talk and to be listened to, and that takes time away from whatever else you were doing.

Rest: While you were campaigning, rest was important so that you stayed at the top of your game. The same rules apply now. Your meeting schedule alone demands that you are rested. Here's proof: I've actually seen a committee chairman fall asleep while listening to a citizen give testimony to a committee. It was a huge embarrassment for everyone on the committee.

Food Intake: Do you remember the term "Freshman Fifteen" from college? Well, first-year elected-officeholders also need to be aware of the tendency to overeat at meetings and events. Many first-term officeholders have been known to add pounds. Eat smaller portions. When you've got several events in a row to attend, eat an appetizer at the first one, and a second appetizer at the second event, then a main-course plate at the third event, and if you have a fourth event you may choose to eat a small dessert. Be vigilant or you're guaranteed to gain weight.

Exercise: Follow your routine. If you used to exercise, keep doing it. If you never followed a steady exercise routine, walk as many places as you can, take the stairs instead of elevators, and walk to off-site meetings when possible.

Be sure to make time for yourself and your family. Schedule family days, sports outings, spa time, time with friends, or whatever you like doing to rejuvenate. You are in control of your schedule.

Why "Part-Time" Positions Are Rarely Part-Time

There is so much to learn with every elected position that you'll quickly find "part-time" elected offices, when you serve in them well, are really not part time. There is a great deal of reading to do: official memos and documents; informal community reading to gather information; government-related reading that informs you about what other agencies like yours are doing so that you can gather ideas and best practices; and, of course, constituent mail and email.

Meeting schedules also keep all elected officeholders busy. There is the preparation reading, the meeting itself—which may last one to ten hours—and the follow-up work and research. People testifying, asking questions, arriving early to try to talk, and staying after meetings to talk can consume additional hours. One-on-one meetings to build agency partnerships take time. Group meetings take time. So does attending the meetings of trade groups, citizen interest groups, and civic groups to learn and to field questions.

Depending on the part-time position to which you have been elected, you may have a team of people to manage. For instance, mayors have other elected officials to lead, the elected and/or appointed council members to lead, and all of the paid staff, which can be as few as two part-time people in rural towns or as many as several thousand employees in metropolitan cities and suburbs.

Generally, voters and constituents forget that most elected positions are not full-time and are not filled with politicians, but rather are filled with people still working their full-time jobs and who are public servants for the greater good of the community. The people we tend to hear about are the politicians, the wrong-doers, the not-doers, and the headline grabbers. Remember the City of Bell's 2010 debacle over outrageous salaries for council members and the mayor: proof that YOU need to run for office so that self-serving individuals don't completely capture government.

Working with Your New Staff

First, your elected office staff is NOT your campaign staff. Government and agency dollars are never to be used for campaign purposes or activities. Get the details from your agency so that you can stay on top of the rules and follow them.

Some elected positions have dedicated full-time staff. Other elected positions have access to shared staff time. Still others have no staff support at all. Your goal will be to build positive working relationships with everyone in the agency so that you can receive help on a daily or as-needed basis. Some of the additional skills that you will benefit from mastering include:

Time Management: Set the hours you are able to work the elected position. Stick to the boundaries and limits you set. You may be able to ask staff to help with the scheduling of your time, or you may have to keep your own calendar and make all of your own RSVP or decline-the-event phone calls. Remember to record all of the events, activities, and meetings on to your calendar so that you don't miss anything that you've committed to attending.

Work Management: Research, policy proposals, scheduling, phone calls, constituent responses, and meetings all comprise your work. Learn what your resources are and what you can ask staff members to do. Discover whom to go to for information and who will actually perform work on your behalf.

Document Handling: Determine what gets a response, what gets shredded, what gets kept, and what is subject to public record laws. The easiest plan is to treat everything you touch as a public record.

Delegation: Do you know which direction to turn to get information on roads? Education? Transportation? Sewage treatment? Labor disputes? Paid legal holidays? Budgeting? Or the thousands of other topics you may be asked about on any given day? Start by asking around and by calling the numbers given in your official directories. Figure out who the key personnel are for sourcing relevant information and getting help. Build cordial relationships with them and add them to your A-list of whom to call about what.

The names on your running list will effectively serve as your pick-up team of experts for special research and referral.

▓ **Note** Your campaign staff is NOT your elected-office staff. Check the laws governing staffing.

Deliver on Your Promises

If you said you'd lower taxes, then your votes need to reflect that. If you said you'd fight crime, then your proposals and votes need to demonstrate action toward reducing crime. If you said you'd work for transparency and account-ability in government, begin by being open and accountable yourself and then working on policies that ensure government transparency. If you said you'd establish a park, then do so.

If you discover that a promise you made was unrealistic, know why it is un-realistic. Be able to show what you learned about the reality of the elected office and the agency of which you are now a part. Be able to show what you've done instead of what you originally set out to do. If you make a new promise, without having at least tried to deliver on your first one and then actually delivered the next best thing, no one will believe you.

Another kind of promise by which you are bound as an elected official is your commitment to attend an event or a meeting. The reason you have to think hard before committing is that you are obliged to actually show up once you've accepted. While serving as a state representative, I'd often hear when I arrived at an event: "You actually came!" I would reply, "Yes, I at-tend the things I say I'll attend. Why?" Each time I'd hear, "Oh, your district counterpart always says she'll attend our event, but then doesn't show up." Guard your reputation! If you say you'll attend, then show up. If you say you will attend, only to discover that you can't, let the hosting organization know as soon as possible. They've gone to great lengths to provide space, food, and information for you, and perhaps they've featured you in their publicity for the event. The least you should do is to be honest, courteous, and conscientious.

Use the Skills You Gained on the Campaign Trail

You spent months building skills on the campaign trail. Bring all of these skills to bear on your new position. Keep building those skills too, so that when you have the elected job and another campaign to manage, you can accomplish both jobs to the level of detail each deserves. Some of the skills you should have in hand include:

Time Management: Use your best time management skills every day.

Meeting People: Keep smiling, keep shaking hands, and keep listening. People still want to be heard more than they want to listen to you talk about what you are doing or going to do.

Pinpointing Constituent Concerns: Distill from all your oral and written communications with your constituents the trends and topics that keep coming up, as well one-off concerns that you suspect might exemplify more general concerns in your constituency. Once you've identified a concern, identify who can help you solve it or craft a policy to solve it.

Setting a vision or plan: A part of why you were elected was the vision and plans you shared while campaigning. Discover what you must do and with whom you will work to implement the vision and to create policies that will make the plans work. Just as in campaigning, you will need a networked and knowledgeable team to transform your vision into action.

Note Keep listening to and for constituent concerns.

Associations and Other Information Sources

In order to stay informed, you will find it helpful to subscribe to professional periodicals and to join several professional associations. GOVERNING magazine is one of my favorite publications for municipal and state governments. It provides stories of best practices, efforts that went awry, lessons, and new information databases and resources.

Professional associations of interest include chambers of commerce, trade or industry associations, or education association groups. The key is to select the one or two organizations from which you will learn the most and meet the most helpful people. You will certainly not have time to attend a dozen association groups' meetings on top of your elected official meetings. Note that when you are asked to serve on an association committee in your elected official capacity you are generally not expected to pay association dues to become a member.

You may have to pay out of your pocket, or the elected body or agency of which you are a part may pay group dues out of its budget. Either way, be sure you know what the laws are governing the payments of membership dues. Dues range from fifty to several thousand dollars per year. Trade associations are typically fifty to several hundred dollars a year, whereas national governmental associations range from several hundred dollars a year to several thousand dollars a year.

Keeping the Structure Alive for a Future Race

As Chapter 12 urged, thank all your campaign volunteers and donors for their support as soon as your race is over. Then stay in touch with them. Let them know how you'll be spending your time going forward and what you are doing to realize the vision they shared with you during your campaign.

▓ **Note** Remember to keep your elected office and campaign activities completely separate.

Conclusion

Strike a healthy balance for your elected, work, and personal lives. Make a difference where you can. The political process wants to move slowly and yet it doesn't always have to. Keep your campaign goals in mind and deliver on your promises, day after day after day.

Congratulations! You've won!

Lose

Congratulations may still be in order. Mostly, though, it feels rotten to lose. All of your hard work didn't earn the votes you needed to win. You, your family, and your volunteers are tired and let down. (If the real reason you ran was to make a point, not to win, then you finished the race where you predicted you would.)

Strangely, when you lose, people are more likely to ask, "Are you going to run again?" My only explanation for this is that when you win, people expect and even assume that you will run again. When you lose, people seem to wonder whether you'll try again and ask the question out loud. It means that you are reminded on a weekly, and eventually, annual basis that there are people who do want you to run again.

The day after I lost my re-election bid for the Idaho House seat I had held for one term, I heard a song on the radio that said something about never giving up and that we all just want to be heard. It lifted my spirits. That same day, I saw a custom license plate in a parking lot that said "NVRQUIT" which made me smile. I chose to think that there is a divine source offering up signs of encouragement right when we need them, if only we're paying attention. Yet, for about two months, I found it difficult to fall asleep each night because of my sadness and frustration over having lost the race when I knew I was doing a good, thorough, and effective job. However, when members of your own party decide to vote for the opposite party to unseat you for whatever real, imagined, or politically motivated controlling reasons, on top of the opposition party working hard to unseat you in a year when dissatisfaction with your party's White House incumbent is at a record high, well, you lose. For as long as two years after the loss, there were times that I'd be driving and feel a pang of frustration about the loss of the race.

I've found that both predictable and strange things can trigger frustrations over an election loss. Predictably, reading about the winner and his/her work that is not being done in the manner in which I know I would be doing it, makes me angry and sad. Strangely, there are also times when for no apparent reason you may become angry. It happens; don't dwell on it. Remember to let yourself grieve without becoming permanently bitter.

Find productive ways to express your ideas, concerns, and hopes. In the end, it is your choice whether you'll stay mired in disappointment and frustration or move forward gracefully and hopefully, buoyed by the support of family, friends and faith. Let only your closest of family members and friends know what your real frustrations are. Your heart and soul will need protected conversation, occasional venting, and time to restore your energies for a future run for office.

If this was your first time out, people may say, "Run again—you built name recognition this time. Sometimes it takes multiple runs to win." Smile through these well-meaning but painful comments. Only your family and you know what you invested in the race and how much it cost you physically, mentally, emotionally, and financially. Smile anyway and say something gracious like "We'll see" or "Stay tuned" or "It's too soon to make that decision." Leave your options open and keep smiling.

If this was a loss after serving in office, then the disappointment is even bigger. You ran again believing that you were doing a good job and should be re-elected. Give yourself time to grieve, without becoming bitter. Some days this is more difficult than others, when you know the winner is not doing the job you were doing. Allow yourself to feel frustrated without taking your frustrations out on the people around you. Find healthy outlets for your grief and frustration.

If this loss was yet another loss after never winning before, allow yourself recovery time. Assess whether you are a message candidate who may never win, and whether you are okay with this. Assess whether you are done this time or whether you'll make different position and campaign strategy choices so that you can create a win for yourself.

When you think you have put the race behind you, sure enough, someone will ask you when you are running again. Or, another person will ask if you are running "next year"—which is not the cycle for most races, as most are two, four, or six year race cycles. This demands a smile, and your still-a-candidate behavioral response to provide education about when the next election year will be for that seat.

I've heard the sayings "No one is a loser until completely giving up" and "Losers are people who are so petrified of not winning they don't even try." In the case of running for office, I think this means that we are not losers unless we decide to stop standing up tall in the community for what we believe is important and to stop working for positive changes—whether that is running for office again or choosing other ways to contribute to the world. Every positive contribution counts.

Learn from Hindsight

You've worked hard, researched much, and listened diligently. Keep applying your research and listening skills so that you can rest happily, having done everything you possibly could have, or so that you can uncover what might have made a difference and created a win for you. Win or lose, include the following elements in your hindsight review:

Study the Numbers: About ten days after most elections, the final vote counts are registered and available for public review. Conduct your research to see which precincts you won and which you lost. Determine what happened demographically and who your best voters were. Identify where you were well received and where you'll need to work harder when you run again.

Review What Part of Your Plan Worked: You'll want to remember what worked so that you can replicate the tasks, activities, and assignments in a future race.

Figure Out What Part of Your Plan Didn't Work: Make notes as soon as you can, while your memory is fresh. It may be painful, but the notes will come in handy when and if you decide to run again.

Identify What You'll Do Differently Next Time: Again, make notes as soon as you can. Right now is when the lessons start to become clear. Keep taking notes as additional do-it-differently ideas arise.

Pinpoint Whether There Was Anything You Could Have Done Differently: Sometimes there is truly nothing that you could have done differently that would have produced a different outcome. The year I lost in the Idaho House race, fellow Republicans were mad at me for some of my votes, Democrats wanted the seat, and the district I represented reflected the national disenchantment with a deeply unpopular Republican president. I had plenty of money for the race, had done my job well, and served the district well: it simply wasn't enough. During the Idaho gubernatorial race four years later, the state as a whole was now disenchanted with a Democratic president and fearful that "wasting" votes for an independent might put a Democrat into the governor's seat. In addition, the media scandalously misserved Idaho voters. Their policy was to report the contest as though it were simply a two-party race. Even if I'd had two million dollars more than the winner to spend on the campaign, 2010 was not the year an independent could win the seat for Idaho governor. People did tell me this throughout the race. Yet the polling surveys repeatedly suggested that an independent could win—with the top three candidates all breaking the 30 percent threshold. In the end, however, the vote tally for the top three diverged to 60, 30, and 6 percent. Like life, election results are not within our control.

Learn what you can from the people in the community whom you had hoped to serve. Ask them what they felt worked about your campaign and what didn't work. Ask them what they think might have worked better.

Gear Up to Run Again

Take at least one month off before deciding to run again. Put all campaign items into boxes so you can sort them after you've decided whether you'll run again or not. Here's what to keep: everything at first. When you are ready, and as you sort the boxes, keep: your lists, all of them; your literature, examples of all of it; your yard signs, which are reusable; and, most importantly of all, keep your sense of humor and your smile.

Also, stay in shape, and stay on top of issues. People will continue to ask what you think about community issues whether you run again or not.

Watch the election cycles to see where and when you'll choose to run again. Assess your personal and professional goals to determine what timing is right for another run.

How Long Does It Take to Recover from Losing a Race?

Everyone's recovery from a loss is different and lasts for a varying amount of time. I met a person who, thirty years after an election loss that was followed by a successful career, still feels a deep dark hole of sadness about it. Early in my gubernatorial campaign, this person warned me: "When you lose this race, because you will, you will be alone and naked standing in the wind." As I recall this encounter, I feel renewed sadness for the person whose pain from an old wound remains so fresh. The message to me was clear: value your family and friends more than you value winning the race; take care of your personal relationships so they'll take care of you.

The day after my gubernatorial loss, I took my seven-year-old to a rollicking children's movie with a Swing Time-like soundtrack, including Bing Crosby's rendition of "The Best Things in Life Are Free" and Harry Roy's performance of "Pick Yourself Up." We had the good fortune of being the only two patrons in the entire theater. Sitting in the middle of the theater, we felt like we were at a private screening. At one point, my musically inclined child sashayed up to the front of the theater and began dancing, wild-crazy, want-to-be-in-the-movie dancing. I hope to always remember what I thought as I sat there: "I am the richest person I know." It was a priceless moment of childlike joy that illuminated one of my darkest hours of sadness and frustration, and restored my perspective after the tunnel vision of the long campaign.

Questions to Help You Determine What You Learned

Ask yourself two overarching questions: "What did I learn?" and "Do I have any regrets?" Then ask yourself questions about the following specific areas:

Issues: What do you now know? Are there other ways that you can still effect positive changes? What can you do to inform and educate others about what you've learned?

District Understanding: Do you know what matters to the people in your district? What will you share and what will you encourage from here?

Politics: What did you learn about your place on the political spectrum? About your relationship with the party you ran with? About your district and how they felt about the party you ran with?

Campaign Strategy: What worked? What didn't? What can be improved and whom can you count on for help in the future?

Volunteers: Who was good at what? Whom can you count on? Who have you dropped from your list and why?

Fundraising: What worked and what didn't? What must you do differently next time? What will you repeat?

Messaging: Did it reflect you? Did it connect to voters? What would connect better? Will a new message work better for you and will it be true to who you are?

Media: Can you do anything differently? What can you do now to continue to maintain and build a relationship with the media?

Working a Room: How can you apply what you learned? Whom did you meet along the way, and plan to keep in conversation with him or her?

You and Your Personal Style: Take time to reflect on these questions in order to find what was good and even great about investing your life in a campaign.

- What did you like about the campaign process?
- What didn't you like?
- Whom do you now know you can count on to support you?
- What did you learn about your energy level and how to maintain it?
- What is your family's commitment to and tolerance of the campaign process?
- Who are your real friends and in what ways did they support you?
- Who are the people you learned are not trustworthy?
- Where can you see that the very act of your vying as a candidate made the whole race a better, tougher, and a more accountable exercise of the democratic process?

Clean Up and Close Out Your Campaign

Store what you plan to keep. At first, your best bet is to store everything and wait until the rawness of the loss has passed before trashing things that you may later wish you had kept. Recycle the papers that you can.

Documentation and Treasurer's Records: Turn all final reports in to the election office. Keep a file in case of audit or if questions arise.

Turn in All Required Reports and Financial Statements by the Election Cycle Close-out Deadline: Determine whether you'll close the campaign account or keep a base amount of funds for a future campaign. Either way, you'll have filings to make with your election office.

Hug Your Family and Friends: Thank them for their cheering and support. Schedule a family vacation that is JUST family so that you all have time to reconnect without cameras, microphones, and outside pressures.

▓ **Note** Remember to thank your family, friends, contributors, and volunteers for all of their support.

Keeping the Structure Alive for a Future Race

Stay in touch with your volunteers and donors. Immediately after the race is over, thank everyone for his support. Let them know how you'll be spending your time going forward. Emails and letters are great ways to communicate. If you had particularly strong supporters, you may want to make phone calls to them and say thank you in person.

Consider keeping your website up as a placeholder for potential future races. Pay for this out of your personal funds. Also, keep your social media outlets alive. The people who voted for you, and maybe even those who voted against you, still care about what you have to say. They'll want to know if you decide to run again. With your boxes of lists and campaign materials safely stored, you can decide at any time to jump back in to run for an elected office.

▓ **Note** An election loss does not make you a loser! Losers are made in their own minds.

Conclusion

Losses are never easy to get over, if you entered the race to win. Ten months after the 2010 gubernatorial election loss, I was stirred out of my last bit of lingering reverie, upon reading President Theodore Roosevelt's rousing rally in his speech to the Sorbonne in 1910: "It is not the critic who counts; not the man who points out how the strong man stumbles, or where the doer of deeds could have done them better. The credit belongs to the man who is actually in the arena, whose face is marred by dust and sweat and blood; who strives valiantly; who errs, who comes short again and again, because there is no effort without error and shortcoming; but who does actually strive to do the deeds; who knows great enthusiasms, the great devotions; who spends himself in a worthy cause; who at the best knows in the end the triumph of high achievement, and who at the worst, if he fails, at least fails while daring greatly, so that his place shall never be with those cold and timid souls who neither know victory nor defeat."

You have dared greatly! Wipe off the dust and sweat. Rest for a bit. Then visit the questions of Chapter 15 in order to decide whether you'll run again or not. If you are already committed to running again—well, wipe off the dust and sweat and rest for a bit just the same.

To Run Again—
or Not?

Today is the day after the election. It might not be the best day to decide whether you'll run again. Win or lose, you and your family need time to regroup. Win or lose, you probably need some sleep and some time for yourself, away from shaking hands and responding to media and attacks.

Once you are rested, revisit this chapter and ask yourself the questions in the following section, to determine whether you'll run again.

Decision Criteria You Can Use to Determine Whether to Run Again

Making the decision to run again, whether you won or lost, works best when you've gotten some distance from Election Day. It may take a week, a few years, or some length of time in between until you can honestly look in the mirror and answer the question, "Will I run again? Why?"

Rushing a decision won't make your decision easier. Letting others talk you into or out of another run won't meet your needs because the only people who understand what it takes to run for office are you, your family members, a few friends, and people who have run for office before. You make your own decision about running again. Conduct some research, reflect on some key questions, and make your own decision.

Research you can conduct includes the following key areas:

- *Review the Numbers*: Get the final vote counts and details from your election office. Run the analysis to learn which areas and precincts you won, which you lost, and identify some reasons as to why. What could have been done differently, if anything?

- *Look at the Party You Chose and the Demographics of Your District*: What party does your district tend to vote for year after year? Will this affect how you'll run or what you'll run for in the future?

- *Reconsider the Position for Which You Ran*: Is it the best match for you and your skills and knowledge? Knowing what you know now, revisit the first chapters of this book to read with fresh eyes and new knowledge what another run for office might look like for you.

Questions you should ask yourself include the following:

- *Did a Good Person Win and Will She Do a Good Job?* If so, maybe you'll decide to wait for the seat to be open, or to run for a completely different office.

- *Do I Still Have the Energy and Passion to Run Again?* Only you can answer this question. No one else really knows or can know how you feel.

- *Did the Campaign Deplete My Finances or Do I Have a Viable Personal, Professional, and Campaign Financial Base to Begin Again?* Once more, only you know the answer. Your campaign treasurer and personal accountant or financial team can weigh in with information, so ask them their view of the situation.

- *After Holding the Office for One or More Terms, Have You Accomplished What You Originally Set Out to Do as a Public Servant in Elected Office?* If so, maybe you are done. If not, you still get to determine whether you have had enough or whether you want to keep running.

- *After Holding Office, Are There Still Things You Want to and Can Accomplish?* What are these things? Make a list of all of the things you have accomplished. Now, make a list of all of the things you'd still like to accomplish for the greater good of your community.

- *What Are the Possible Ways, Other Than Holding Elected Office, That You Can Be Involved in Creating Change in the Community or in the Country?* Elected office is just one way to serve. Consider pursuing appointments because they are also great public service and learning opportunities. Or volunteer for other campaigns, boards, and committees to keep your hand in what is going on in the community. You have options.

Note Make your own decision about running again.

In 2006, for all the reasons you've already read about, I lost the re-election bid to a lawyer who then got re-elected; then got elected to the Senate; and then got placed in the Senate's minority leadership team. The best person does not always win elections. Maybe the right thing works out, but truly the best people for the work that needs to be done are not always the ones who win races. So, pick yourself up, and do something you know you are good at before deciding whether you will run again.

Two weeks after the 2006 election, I met with a public official who had held a succession of elected offices in Idaho for twenty-six years, despite a painful loss early in his political career. I wanted to ask him for some input about running again. Here's what he told me: "Well, Jana, right now asking the question about running again is like asking a woman who's just given birth whether she's ready to have another baby." Frankly, it wasn't a terribly helpful analogy because I've never given birth. Nonetheless, I took his message— "It's too soon to decide; give yourself some time"—to heart. In 2009, after reflection and deliberation, I decided to run for office against the very person who had offered up this obstetric simile. I ran against him because I didn't see him doing the job he'd promised to do, and I knew for certain—and still know—that I could do a better job.

Do You Still Have Your Passion?

After a tough pair of wins in the 2004 primary and general elections, I was exhilarated and honored to be sworn in as an elected official. My mindset was and continues to be one of public servant rather than politician, and I continue to educate people about the difference. My term in office was educational and life-changing for me and for those whom I served, as the work I did made an impact on education, local government, and economic development for our state. As a result of my championing the growth of new business sectors in Idaho, new trade groups grew up to carry on the work I had begun. Additionally, I believe that the soundly researched and difficult questions that I politely but persistently asked in legislative session during my term positively impacted the statehouse's political culture. Fellow legislators, people testifying before the legislature, my constituents, and the general public witnessed a legislator who was unafraid to take the heat for asking hard questions in the public interest. Finally, laws were changed for the better because of my service.

Despite all these positive outcomes, I can also say that I was continually frustrated by the political ethos of backroom maneuvering and dealmaking in the state house; by the deceits casually practiced by elected officials and their staffs and by lobbyists; by the tolerance of expedient decisions and sloppy communications among elected officials; and by the cynical and undemocratic working assumption of many veteran legislators that "voters aren't that smart."

In 2006, after weeks of attack by lobbyists, a committee chairman, and governor's staff on nearly all the initiatives on which I was working, I felt so disgusted and exhausted that I approached a veteran colleague for insight. I asked her, "When it is this brutal, what makes you keep coming back?" She answered, "Because I know I am the best person from my district to do this job." That's conviction. That's commitment. Over the years, I've heard many other elected officeholders say, "This is the best job I've ever had. I love it." That's the passion that feeds the desire to keep on running.

After losing the 2010 race for governor, I moved on quickly to planning what I would do next with my business, my educational pursuits, and the shutdown of my campaign. Then I took a week-long, family-only trip. We had a great time reconnecting as a family, unfettered by the campaign trail and the campaign schedule.

Some days I feel the passion welling up for another run for elected office. Other days I feel frustrated. Some days I realize that even if I never gave another volunteer hour to the community for the rest of my life, I'd already have given plenty and served well. Other days I am ready to jump in and lead causes, from economic development to protecting children and their well-being. Some days I am uniquely focused on my family. Other days I am focused as well on all of the challenges this country faces at every level when lack of vision and lack of leadership prevail.

You too may feel these back-and-forth swings, whether you won or lost. It is normal for intelligent and thoughtful people to keep observing the world around them and to keep reflecting upon our roles in our communities and the world.

Dispassionately take your post-election temperature. Are you still passionate enough about holding an elected office as a vehicle for effecting change in your community to run again? If you are, great! Your supporters are likely to support you again.

If you are not, that can be great, too, because maybe there is another and possibly more effective way for you to contribute to the fabric of your community. Explore the possibilities of serving in appointed positions that implement policies, rules, and laws. Discover whether a different position might be a better match for your talents and time. Ask people lots of questions about their take on what happened in the election. Then ask yourself again, "Do I still have enough passion to run again for office?"

Gearing Up to Run Again

You've kept your lists, literature, yard signs, and smile. Now, stay in shape, on top of the issues, and on top of your game!

You've kept this book. Begin again with Chapter 2 and work your way through your messaging, planning, and budgeting. Rebuild your volunteer team and focus on the goal of winning so that you can serve in public office.

Once you decide to run again, reconnect with your previous supporters, volunteers, and campaign contributors. They should hear from you first that you are running again. You'll want to invite them to support you again.

The treadmill of running for elected office can get easier when you run for the same office. You can remobilize a great volunteer team to support all of the behind-the-scenes work that must be done year over year to ensure election victories.

Gearing Down to Purge the Urge

What do you want to do? What does your family want you to do? Many conversations, many months of reflection, and many months of alternative work may be needed before you and your family can make the decision about your running again. Allow yourself the necessary time. You want to be really sure you are done running before making an announcement that will impel your supporters to look for a new champion.

If you arrive at the decision that you are done running for office, you are done. You can take pride in yourself that you've served your community and country by the very act of running or holding an elected office. If people were to stop running, the American system of government would collapse. Your commitment to run would help keep our democracy working. On the other hand, your decision to stop running might keep you from losing your family, your full-time job, your professional career, your quality of life, or your mind.

You are the only one who can make the decision about running again. Your health may dictate an answer, yet plenty of people in poor health hold elected office. Your family may wish you wouldn't ever run again, yet you are the one to determine what will be a good action plan for your family and your community. You are the only one who feels what you feel and knows whether you've got the depth of passion to see you through another campaign. You decide.

If you just can't purge your urge to run, consider gearing up to run again, for the same or a different office. Be aware that multiple runs for the same or different offices without ever winning can ultimately lead to your being disparagingly pigeonholed as a "perennial candidate"—a symbolic sideshow or habitual fixture rather than a serious contender.

▓ **Note** You are the only one who can make the decision about running again.

Conclusion

You've run the race. You've contributed to the representative democratic fabric of America. If you choose not to run again, you've tried, you've learned, and your very act of participating in the race with all your might *did* make a difference. If you choose to run again, remember all that you've learned, all the people you have met, and all of the people who helped you along the way. America needs public servants—people who genuinely care about the people and communities around them!

Our communities, states, and nation need people to run for elected office who are virtuous and energetic and who care deeply about process and issues. The voters in your community need you, even if they haven't yet figured out how much they need you. Your children's and grandchildren's generations need you, too: your foresight, your care, your molding influence on long-reaching policy, and your modeling of the conduct of a citizen who embraces her democratic duty.

May you be blessed in all that you do and pursue. May your family and friends continue to stand with you, supporting and cheering your fight to represent them and to help make their community and country as great as they can be. Remember: only civic-minded individuals such as YOU have the stuff to become the public servants who can preserve our republic and lead America into greatness.

Index

CPSIA information can be obtained at www.ICGtesting.com
Printed in the USA
LVOW080354301211

261706LV00001B/96/P